Marinella Perroni

KERYGMA AND PROPHECY

Pope Francis' Biblical Hermeneutics

LIBERIA EDITRICE VATICANA

Published in Australia by

© Copyright 2019 Coventry Press

Coventry Press
33 Scoresby Road
Bayswater Vic. 3153
Australia

Translated into English by Salesians Of Don Bosco of the Province of Mary Help Of Christians of Australia and The Pacific

ISBN 9780987643155

© Copyright 2017 - Libreria Editrice Vaticana
00120 Città del Vaticano
Tel. 06.698.81032 - Fax 06.698.84716
commerciale.lev@spc.va

All rights reserved. Other than for the purposes and subject to the conditions prescribed under the *Copyright Act*, no part of this publication may be reproduced, stored in a retrieval system, or transmitted in any form or by any means, electronic, mechanical, photocopying, recording or otherwise, without the prior permission of the publisher.

Cataloguing-in-Publication entry is available from the National Library of Australia http:/catalogue.nla.gov.au/.

Printed in Australia

www.coventrypress.com.au

SERIES
THE THEOLOGY OF POPE FRANCIS

- JURGEN WERBICK: *God's weakness for humankind.* Pope Francis' view of God

- LUCIO CASULA: *Faces, gestures and places.* Pope Francis' Christology

- PETER HÜNERMANN: *Human beings according to Christ today.* Pope Francis' Anthropology

- ROBERTO REPOLE: *The dream of a gospel-inspired Church.* Pope Francis' Ecclesiology

- CARLOS GALLI: *Christ, Mary, the Church and the peoples.* Pope Francis' Mariology

- SANTIAGO MADRIGAL TERRAZAS: *'Unity Prevails over Conflict'.* Pope Francis' Ecumenism

- ARISTIDE FUMAGALLI: *Journeying in love.* Pope Francis' Moral Theology

- JUAN CARLOS SCANNONE: *The Gospel of Mercy in the spirit of discernment.* Pope Francis' Social Ethics

- MARINELLA PERRONI: *Kerygma and prophecy.* Pope Francis' Biblical Hermeneutics

- PIERO CODA: *'The Church is the Gospel'.* At the sources of Pope Francis' theology

- MARKO IVAN RUPNIK: *According to the Spirit.* Spiritual theology on the move with Pope Francis' Church

ABBREVIATIONS

AL *Amoris Laetitia*

EG *Evangelii Gaudium*

EN *Evangelii Nuntiandi*

GS *Gaudium et Spes*

LG *Lumen Gentium*

LS *Laudato Si'*

MeM *Misericordia et Misera*

RS *Ratio Studiorum*

PREFACE TO THE SERIES

From the time of his first appearance in St Peter's Square on the evening of his election, it was more than clear that Francis' pontificate would be adopting a new style. His modest apparel, calling himself the Bishop of Rome, asking the people to pray for him – in the 'deafening silence' of a packed square – and greeting them with a simple '*buonasera*' (good evening) … these were all eloquent signs of the fact that there was a change taking place in the way the Pope related to people, and thus in the 'language' used.

The gestures and words that have followed from that occasion only confirm and strengthen this first impression. Indeed, it could be said that over the ensuing years, the image of the papacy has been decidedly transformed, involving a change that affects homilies, addresses and documents promulgated as well.

As could be predicted, this has generated divergent opinions, especially regarding his teaching. While many have in fact welcomes his magisterium with enthusiasm and deep interest, sensing the fresh wind of the gospel, some others have approached it in a more detached way and, at times, with suspicion. There has been no lack of more absolute views, even going as far as to doubt the existence of a theology in Francis' teaching.

A summary judgement of this kind could come from the very different backgrounds of Francis and his predecessor, Benedict XVI. The latter, we know, has been one of the most outstanding and important theologians of the twentieth century and undoubtedly relied on his personal theological development in his rich papal magisterium. We have not yet fully appreciated, nor will we cease to appreciate, the depth of this magisterium. What Bergoglio has behind him, on the other hand, is his long and deep-rooted experience as a religious and a pastor.

However, this does not mean that his magisterium is without a theology. The fact that he was not mostly, or only, a 'professional' theologian does not mean that his magisterium is not supported by a theology. Were this the case, we could say that, strictly speaking, the majority of his predecessors were without a theology, given that Ratzinger represents the exception rather than the rule.

In any case, the fact that we can discuss the theological significance of Francis' magisterium, as well as the fact that, very often, some of his highly evocative and very immediate expressions have been so abused as to rob them of their profundity – in the journalistic as well as the ecclesial ambit – makes the response of this series, which I have the honour of presenting, a significant one.

By drawing on the competence and rigorous study of theologians of proven worth, coming from diverse contexts, the series has sought to research the theological thinking which supports the Pope's teaching. It explores its roots, its freshness, and its continuity with earlier magisterium.

The result can be found in the eleven volumes which make up this series with its simple and direct title: 'The Theology of Pope Francis'.

They can be read independently of one another, obviously; they have been written by individual authors independently of each other. Nevertheless, the hope is that a reading of the entire series would not only be a valuable aid for grasping the theology upon which Francis' teaching is based, in the various theological fields of knowledge, but also an introduction to the key points of his thinking and teaching overall.

The intention, then, is not one of 'apologetics', and even less so is it to add further voices to the many already speaking about the Pope. The aim is to try to see, and to help others to see, what theological thinking Francis bases himself on and expresses, in such a fresh way in his teaching.

Among the many discoveries the reader could make in reading these volumes, would certainly be that of observing how so much of the beneficial freshness of the Council's teaching flows into Francis' magisterium. This is true both of the theological preparation he has had, and of what has followed from it. Given that it is perhaps still too soon for all this wealth to become common patrimony, peacefully and fully received by everyone, it should be no surprise that the Pope's teaching is sometimes not immediately understood by everyone.

By the same token, a point of no return has been reached in Francis' teaching, one that recent theology and the Council have both taught: that doctrine cannot be something extraneous to so-called pastoral theology and ministry. The truth that the Church is called to watch over is the truth of Christ's Gospel, which needs to be communicated to the women and men of every time and place. This is why the task of the ecclesial magisterium must also be one of favouring this communication of the Gospel. Hence, theology can never be reduced to a dry, desk-bound exercise, disconnected from the life of the people of God and its mission. This mission is that the women and men of every age encounter the perennial and inexhaustible freshness of Jesus' Gospel.

Over these years there have been those who have heard some of Francis' own critical statements regarding theology or theologians, and have concluded that he holds it and them in low esteem. Perhaps a more detailed study of the Pope's teaching, such as offered by this series, could also be helpful for showing that, while we always need to be critical of a theology that loses its vital connection to the living faith of the Church, it is also essential to have a theology which takes up the task of thinking critically about this very faith, and doing so with 'creative fidelity', so that it may continue to be proclaimed.

Francis' teaching is certainly not lacking in a theology of this kind; and a theology of the kind is certainly one much desired by a magisterium such as his, which so wants God's mercy to continue to touch the minds and hearts of the women and men of our time.

Editor-in-chief
ROBERTO REPOLE

CONTENTS

Abbreviations 4
Preface to the Series 5
Introduction 11

Chapter I

POPE FRANCIS' BIBLICAL HERMENEUTICS 17

1. Identifying the salient features of the biblical fabric as a whole 17

2. Biblical theology and hermeneutics: an inseparable pair today 21

    2.1. Between history and theology 24

    2.2. The new hermenutics 31

3. A kerygmatic purpose and a prophetic vigour 35

    3.1. A theology 'from the end of the world'. 38

    3.2. Inculturation of the gospel 42

    3.3. A deuteronomic memory 47

4. Ignatian roots 51

    4.1. The spirituality of the *Exercises* 52

    4.2. The pedagogical method of the *Ratio Studiorum* 61

5. *Reception of the Council* 63
6. *The service of the Word* 67

Chapter 2

Gaudium, Laus, Laetitia, Misericordia 73

1. *A canon within the canon* 73
2. *Evangelii Gaudium's* hymn to joy 77
   2.1. From prophetic hope to the messianic present 79
   2.2. The joy of messianic proclamation ... 82
3. *Laudato Si': The world's joyful mystery* 85
4. *Amoris Laetitia:* why love is a joy 90
5. *Misericordia et Misera:* This is the time for mercy 95

In Conclusion 101

INTRODUCTION

It would be good to be clear from the outset that we have no desire to take part in the debate over everything Pope Francis has said and done since the day of his election. Nor do we wish to take a stance, whatever that may be, regarding this. It is true, of course, that Francis' pontificate has been 'on display' from the very beginning and many, competent or otherwise, have thought it good to speak out, judging his every word, choice and gesture. At times, their fury has been curious given that Francis wants freedom of speech to reign in his Church, and that during this period, no theologian has been rebuked or alienated. No one, theologian or not, has been silenced; the only thing asked of people is that they accept the rules of a plurality of viewpoints. On the other hand, there is an increasing number of books on 'his' theology, as if testimony to the fact that one can pay attention to it and make it the object of reflection, even without needing to dedicate a PhD to it or publish an *Opera Omnia*.

Beyond any controversy, but also without any apologetic intent, we would like to reflect in these pages on one of the dimensions that characterizes this pontificate. It is a very specific dimension – the weight Francis gives to Scripture in carrying out the Petrine ministry as he would strongly like that ministry to be, a ministry of unity and, for the world, a ministry of hope. So in short, we would like to ask ourselves how, over these early years of his pontificate, Francis has guided the Church entrusted to him to enter into the mystery of the Scriptures, making them its daily bread but also bread which is broken and shared.

It might seem inappropriate to speak of Francis' 'biblical theology'. Francis has never kept his reservations about theologians a secret, nor has he ever claimed to present himself to the Church and the world as a professional theologian. He studied theology, even at length, given his choice to join the Society of Jesus; he also taught it for a time, but renounced pursuit of a doctorate and did not make teaching his life's choice. He has always interpreted his ecclesial belonging and the exercising of the various functions and ministries he has been called to, in fundamentally pastoral and especially testimonial terms.

Francis' faith, however, is a reasoned faith with strong self-awareness, a theological faith. This does not mean it is not open to question, or that it is incapable of choosing silence when pushed to painful thresholds. It does not mean that it cannot recognise what is unfathomable, and that it does not choose to retreat when confronted by the freedom of someone who wants no knowledge of God or Jesus Christ. It is a stable but not stationary faith, no rock-like theoretical construction made up of ideas and principles. It is peaceful, because it wins out in the daily grind and amid the tides of history, and at times even despite history.[1]

---

[1] It was the great theologian of the Council, Cipriano Vagaggini, who defined theology as 'an operation of the believer in peaceful possession of his faith': *Teologia*, in G BARBAGLIO-S

It is a faith like Abraham's, who 'believed God and it was reckoned to him as righteous' (Rom 4:3); like Moses' faith, who 'persevered as though he saw him who was invisible' (Heb 11:27); like David's, who, despite his sin, knows that his words are those 'of the man whom God exalted, the anointed of the God of Jacob, the favourite of the Strong One of Israel' (2 Sam 23:1); or like the faith of the mother of Samuel, whom Eli, the temple priest, mistook for a drunkard, but who was instead 'pouring out [her] soul before the LORD' (1 Sam 1:12-14). But also like Jesus' faith, who 'although he was a Son, he learned obedience through what he suffered' (Heb 5:8); or Peter's faith, who because of his betrayal 'wept bitterly' (Mt 26:75; Lk 22:62); or again, like the faith of Mary Magdalene or Paul, for whom the basis of their apostolic investiture was their personal encounter with the Risen Christ (Jn 20:18 and Gal 1:15-16).

We could continue to appeal to the 'great cloud of witnesses,' that endless number of women and men who have remained firm in faith throughout three millennia, faith understood as a fundamental decision when faced with life and history.

Francis has accepted the ministry entrusted to him and is carrying it out in the obedience requested of priests: 'Tend the flock of God that is in your charge, exercising the oversight, not under compulsion but willingly, as God would have you do it – not for sordid gain but eagerly. Do not lord it over those in your charge but be examples to your flock' (1 Pet 5:2-3).

DIANICH, *Nuovo Dizionaario di Teologia*, Paoline, Alba, 1977, 1597–1711, 1599.

We will attempt to explore the terms in which Francis' magisterium contains a kind of 'biblical theology', in the first part of this essay of ours. From a general point of view we can already state, however, that his entire magisterium, be it expressed authoritatively in documents, or in his daily homilies, can be reduced to one of the fundamental dimensions of biblical theology, the kerygmatic. Then, if we go to the heart of Francis' magisterium in a more detailed fashion by looking at his Apostolic Exhortation and his Encyclical, it will allow us to focus on the strong points of his Scriptural hermeneutics, or the criteria by which the master of the household of whom Matthew speaks 'brings out of his treasure what is new and what is old' (13:52). They underpin his view of God and the world, his understanding of life and history, other than what is clearly his view of the Church's mission.

It would not only be rash but also foolish, in the end, to claim that we can add it all up. Francis' theology is not tied to academia, nor can it be characterized, like the theology of his immediate predecessors, in doctrinal terms, but it tries to relate to 'The joys and the hopes, the griefs and the anxieties of the men of this age, especially those who are poor or in any way afflicted' *Gaudium et Spes* (*GS*), as a voice of the Church called to live in the world without being of the world. Hence, no different from the Apostle Paul's, it is a theology *in fieri*, strongly linked to the opportunities provided by history. But it is neither fragmented nor fragmentary. As with Paul, this dependence on circumstance does not mean casualness but *kairos*, the right and opportune moment. It is the moment that belongs to God's time, a time of promise and expectation, a time of fulfilment and gratitude, a time of necessity and decision. A time of freedom. It is God's time and that of humankind 'whom he favours' (Lk 20:14).

It is no coincidence that the second dimension which makes Francis' magisterium a form of biblical theology *in fieri* is the prophetic one. Faith in Jesus, the Messiah of God, asks us to be visionaries, as the disciples (men and women) of the Risen Lord were, in continuity with the prophets of Israel. It is not about denying the dark moments of history, but of 'seeing' that God's grace brings a radiance that shines within them, and without fear of admitting that the role of prophecy at the same time establishes its limits: prophecy must prepare for, not lead to, fulfilment. Perhaps in denunciation, and even more strongly in consolation, Francis' magisterium also seeks to be prophetic proclamation, a view of history which, however, moves toward its fulfilment. Jesus and his gospel of mercy are the only and unshakeable guarantee of this. It is in complete continuity, furthermore, with Ignatius' spirituality. The two key words of his episcopal motto (*Miserando atque eligendo*) sum this up firmly. They refer to Matthew's account of the call of Levi the tax collector, and testify to how clearly Francis' call and ministry are rooted in the gospel, and in the spiritual tradition of the Society of Jesus.

Jesus, his person and mission, but also his attitude and behaviour, his words and silences, are the foundation and criteria for Francis' prophetic *kerygma*, which is not circumscribed, as with Paul, by the soteriological and christological confession of the saving value of death and resurrection. Nor for him, on the other hand, is the gospel only the content of Jesus' preaching. That would not have performative power. The gospel is Jesus himself, and our trusting intimacy with him. He, therefore, is the joyful proclamation, the *kerygma*, to be brought to the poor. He is freedom for prisoners, recovery of sight for the blind, freedom for the oppressed (Is 61:1-2 and Lk 4:18-19). It is he who brings the two Testaments together and brings the promise to fulfilment, revealing the true face of the God of mercy. For Francis, this is the theological message handed down to us by the Bible, and thus the core of his theology of the Scriptures.

Chapter 1
POPE FRANCIS' BIBLICAL HERMENEUTICS

Even though Jorge Mario Bergoglio has never claimed to develop his own biblical theology in any systematic kind of way, we have no doubt that both his preaching and magisterium are deeply rooted in his knowledge and interpretation of the Scriptures. A quick overview of the nature, tasks and perspectives of biblical theology could be helpful, both to grasp its intrinsic plurality, especially today with the development of the new hermeneutics, and more specifically to outline Pope Francis' biblical hermeneutics. In this regard, naturally, we are clear that it will be more essential than ever, then, to look at the strong influence Ignatian spirituality has on his theological and biblical outlook. Nor should we forget that although Bergoglio did not attend the Council, he is in complete harmony with the spirit as well as the letter of that ecclesial event. Finally, his daily homiletic practice needs to be considered as the privileged place where his relationship with the Word becomes a *diakonia*, a service, and therefore a high point of his Petrine ministry.

1. *Identifying the salient features of the biblical fabric as a whole*

In general terms, it can be said that the aim of biblical theology is the search for a unified and dynamic view of the message preserved in the Bible. Insofar as it is a collection of writings from eras very far apart from one another, and insofar as it is the expression of different ways of understanding the relationship with the divinity but also of interpreting human history, the Bible can only be a complex composition from various points of view. If we consider them in literary terms, the texts are the result of the interweaving of different traditions and present a variety of genres and forms which need to be evaluated both for their specific nature, and for their possible historical connection with what they are speaking about. On the other hand, there has been many a motivation over the centuries for integrating these traditions into a composite whole and allowing a precise purpose to shine through. There are many traditional elements which subsequent versions have received as more or less explicit expressions of the preparation, birth and development of a people's faith, and this faith gradually assumed authority in these texts, transforming them into a scriptural deposit which becomes the foundation of that faith's identity. The arranging of the Pentateuch, or the bringing together of the psalms into a collection, or the defining of a body of prophetic literature or wisdom material, the reception of the traditions about Jesus in the four Gospels, and the preservation of testimonies in the apostolic tradition, all then coming to a point of canonical definition of writings considered to be foundational both for Judaism and Christianity – all this has contributed to the creation of the great body of Scripture which has gone under the name of the Bible, or 'the books' (*tà biblía*).

There is no doubt, moreover, that a theological character is to be attributed to all the steps, taken as a whole, which led to the body of sacred texts which make up the scriptures of Judaism and Christianity. It is not just a religious character, like so much other literature, because the books of the Bible do not simply transmit an individual or collective experience of the divine in their accounts or verses, but they develop a thought, or rather, an interweaving of thoughts about God, and present the existential and ethical implications of this. It goes further, because they attribute the quality of God's revelation to it. Hence, it is the 'Word of God' for what it says about God but also insofar as it is the word which God himself addresses to his people.

The different ways of interpreting Scripture, developed over the long Christian tradition, have always aimed at favouring an overall interpretation of the Bible which can come to terms with its theological message, rather than looking at the difference between writings and the fragmentation which is the historical and literary problems each text presents if considered individually. Hence, though without falling into over-simplification or being too generic, any biblical theology has always sought interpretative criteria which are pertinent to the nature of these writings and suited to dealing with the biblical message as a whole.

It should also be said, then, that every model of biblical theology is strictly bound up with the historical and cultural context within which it takes shape. It is sufficient to consider, for example, one of the themes and vital problems of any interpretation of the Bible as a whole, which is the relationship between the Old and New Testament and, as a consequence, the question of Jesus' Jewishness and its implications. In times when an anti-Jewish spirit reigned, such problems were tackled differently than they are today in the light of a new approach to understanding the relationship between Jews and Christians. From a methodological point of view, furthermore, any biblical theology is strongly influenced by the theories of knowledge of its own time. So what is true for the understanding of the biblical books is also true for biblical theologies: if each of the books expresses its own theology quite different at times from that of the other books, then the various interpretative models can only but be different, even though they are born of a desire to look beyond the individual differences and many contradictions found in the Bible.

Scripture, then, is already in itself a grand 'fresco' of many theologies, but this does not mean it is devoid of central elements, so we should not be surprised that the entire history of biblical interpretation is not contained just within the work of exegesis of individual texts, but is punctuated by different attempts at identifying the salient features of the Bible taken as a whole. Whence comes the brief history of biblical theology, the discipline which, on the one hand, has taken shape initially from the exegesis of texts, but on the other, has developed in relationship with many new theories of interpretation.

This has been a brief history, but it seemed to us to be important to go back over it.

2. Biblical theology and hermeneutics: an inseparable pair today

The story of Christian biblical hermeneutics, even before biblical theology was defined as an academic discipline, is a complex one. It is also rooted in the biblical tradition itself, formed thanks to a continual process of reception, and forever generating new ones. Was it not, perhaps, a very real 'biblical theology' which the early Jewish-Christians had to do in order to arrive at developing their own faith in Jesus of Nazareth? The evangelists are well aware of this. Luke attests to it in his paradigmatic episode of the two disciples from Emmaus, when he presents the understanding of the Scriptures as a condition for recognizing the Risen Lord (24:45). And John has us understand this when he comments on the early difficulties the disciples had in believing in the resurrection, with the observation: 'They still did not understand the scripture that he must rise from the dead' (20:9).

It is more than clear from all four Gospels, on the other hand, that the development of a christological faith very often begins with reception of the theology of the different biblical books.

Hence, from the outset, since the proclamation of faith in Jesus of Nazareth established the content of the Holy Scriptures as its foundation, a long history of reception began which, at every historical twist and turn, has accompanied the various inculturations of the Christian faith. The Greek and Latin Fathers interpreted the holy books within the perspective of the epistemology of their own culture and, between the 4th and 6th centuries, the great Ecumenical Councils redeveloped the contents of biblical faith in dogmatic formulas constructed according to Greek philosophy. The great theological summaries of the medieval era, by St Thomas Aquinas and St Bonaventure, re-appropriated Aristotelian structure and Platonic understanding respectively. In the 16th century, the Reformation imposed a radical rethinking of the dominant theological structure by affirming the primacy of Scripture, but in the Catholic Church, from the Council of Trent to the so-called neo-scholastic period, a completely functional use of Scripture established itself: without great hermeneutical creativity, theologians used it to mine *dicta probantia*, or in other words, they extrapolated certain testimonies from the different writings, which were understood very literally and could be used to support speculative statements that were too often far removed from the specific meaning of the biblical texts.

Though, up to this point, we can speak of different hermeneutical models through which to offer an interpretation of Scripture texts, the modern era, in connection with the development of the historical and philological sciences, would see a great development of biblical exegesis understood as the science of the study of ancient writings aimed above all at seeking the meaning of the texts on the basis of what their authors intended to communicate to their contemporaries. There were even further gains, mostly among Protestants and only among Catholics from the beginning of the 20th century, in research into the historical dimension of Revelation, which would lead to the recognition of the undeniable differences, sometimes very much pronounced, that exist between the various biblical books and even within them. The problem of different vocabulary and style, but especially of content, which in reality Augustine had already lucidly perceived in relation to the four Gospels,[1] became ever more acute, and the need emerged to coordinate biblical pluralism within a consistent theological perspective. Over the 19th and 20th centuries, it would be the tension between historical research and dogmatic systematization that would lead to animated discussion among scholars.

It is with this background that we must understand the need to enliven a biblical discipline which, without handing the Bible over to dogmatics once more, is configured as a science which is not only historical but theological. Besides, beginning with the 18th century, the term 'hermeneutics' begins to be used by different philosophical schools and theories as a science which researches what the different texts might be saying to the men and women of today. On the other hand, although historico-critical research preserves its own vigour still, and with it, also preserves attention to the historical value of each biblical pericope, new exegetical methods tied especially to the linguistic sciences have assumed the dynamic relationship they establish with the reader as an interpretative criterion.

Currently, it is not easy to arrive at a synthesis between exegesis, biblical theology, and hermeneutics, but it is

---

1 See his work *Harmony of the Gospels*.

essential, in our view, to at least try to explore the fruitful tension which both separates and unites them. In this regard, it could help to briefly look at the history of biblical theology, because it is an academic discipline which is already a science of synthesis. Thus, it allows us to acknowledge how any hermeneutics of biblical texts also presumes the support of an exegetical method on the one hand, and appeals, on the other, to a theological reference model. It is what we will do further on to clarify what Pope Francis' biblical hermeneutics is. It is not a model coming out of nowhere, but is bound up with the history of biblical theology and especially the efforts it has made to respond adequately to the purpose for which it came into being.

2.1 Between history and theology

The need to offer a solution to the problem of the relationship between historical awareness and theoretical need goes back to the 18th century, and a first attempt at developing a biblical theology begins precisely with the definition of the principle of the *oeconomia temporum*.[2] Johann Philipp Gabler would offer a more precise definition in 1787.[3] For him, biblical theology is distinct from dogmatic theology, because of its *historical nature*, given that it passes on what the different hagiographies were gradually able to perceive regarding divine realities. We are only at

[2] J-H Maius, *Oeconomia temporum Veteris testamenti* …, Vol IV, Frankfurt a.M., 1706.
[3] *On the Correct Distinction Between Dogmatic and Biblical Theology and the Right Definition of Their Goals*. The 1787 inaugural address at University of Altdorf. 1 The translation, along with an

the beginning, but already, beyond researching the specific nature of the message of each biblical book, biblical theology begins to grow in its need to identify a consistent unifying principle able to give systematic structure to individual exegetical analyses.[4]

Can biblical theology succeed in creating a bridge between the different theologies found in Holy Scripture with regard to the specific requirements of method demanded by doing theology? A first way of responding to this dilemma was that of considering the biblical theology of the First Covenant independently of the Second Covenant. Three works on the biblical theology of the Old Testament dominated the 19th and 20th centuries: one by Walter Eichrodt,[5] who proposed identifying the unifying core in the notion of Covenant in the Old Testament; another by Gerhard von Rad[6] who, instead, interprets the different threads found there in terms of dynamic development, or in other words, from the theological interpretation of its past by Israel, to the theology of the Prophetic traditions, to a theology of

extensive analysis of its history and significance, originally appeared in John Sandys-Wunsch and Laurence Eldredge, "J. P. Gabler and the Distinction Between Biblical and Dogmatic Theology: Translation, Commentary, and Discussion of His Originality," SJT (Scottish Journal of Theology) 33 (1980): 135-158 (esp. 134-44).

4 HJ KRAUS, G BENZI, 'Teologia biblica', in R. PENNA-G PEREGO-G RAVASI (eds), *Temi teologici della Bibbia*, San Paolo, Cinisello Balsamo 2010, 1383–1395.

5 W EICHRODT, *Theologie des Alten Testament*, Leipzig, 1935 (English translation, Theology of the Old Testament, Westminster John Knox Press, 1961).

6 G VON RAD, *Die Theologie der geschichtlichen Überlieferung Israels*, München, 1957 (English translation, The Theology of

wisdom which finds its specific articulation, consistent with Israelite faith, in the various books of Wisdom literature. Then, more recently, there is the work in several volumes by Rolf Rendtorff. In his *The Old Testament. An Introduction*, he examines the biblical text from the historical and literary point of view, with Israelite social life as the background, while in his two volumes on the *The Canonical Hebrew Bible. Theology of the Old Testament*, he not only calls on the results of modern biblical criticism regarding the *intentio auctoris* of the biblical texts, but integrates them with the history of the process by which they became part of the canon, and finally, he arrives at an outline of the overall fabric of the Old Testament, beginning with its key themes.[7]

Instead, regarding the theology of the New Testament, after the two World Wars it was the work of Rudolf Bultmann[8] which gained prominence. He no longer distinguishes only the theological perspectives proper to each text, but the different levels of theology which led to the formation of the Jesus tradition, that is, the *kerygma* of the early community, the theological themes of Hellenistic

---

Israel's Prophetic Traditions, Westminster John Knox Press, 1960)

7 R Rendtorff, *Das Alte Testament. Eine Einführung*, Neukirchen 1983 (English edition, The Old Testament, An Introduction, Fortress Press, 1 Jan. 1991), and *Theologie des Alten Testaments. Ein kanonischer Entwurf*. I: *Kanonische Grundlegung*; II, *Thematische Entfaltung*, Neukirchen 1999 (English edition, The Canonical Hebrew Bible, The Theology of the Old Testament, Deo Publications, 2005).

8 R Bultmann, *Theologie des Neuen Testaments*, Tübingen, 1958 (English edition, Theology of the New Testament, Baylor University Press, Waco, Texas, 2007).

communities and the theologies of Paul and John. Bultmann's formulation of things became a school of thought as shown by the New Testament biblical theologies of Eduard Lohse[9] and Leonhard Goppelt.[10] But there have also been the great contributions of other scholars like Joachim Jeremias,[11] for example, who identifies the nub of New Testament theology in his critical reconstruction of Jesus' preaching, which is also the criterion for evaluating the apostolic tradition that followed; or Karl Hermann Schelkle,[12] whose encyclopedic work reconstructs the various theological threads found in the Bible, taking account both of their ramifications and their parallels. While respecting the thinking of each biblical author, he presents it in systematic terms, and thus comes to grapple with how the theological unity of Scripture is manifested in the salvific economy of God which embraces the whole of history from creation to eschatology.

We are simply providing some examples here by way of reference: over the period stretching to the second half of the 20th century, biblical theology was profoundly driven by its historical sense, and saw the flourishing of many other outstanding works concerning both Old and New

---

9 E LOHSE, *Grundriss der neutestamentlichen Theologie*, Stuttgart, 1975.

10 L GOPPELT, *Theologie des Neuen Testaments*, (English edition, Theology of the New Testament, W.B. Eerdmans Publishing Company, 1981).

11 J JEREMIAS, *Neutestamentliche Theologie*, Gütersloh, 1971 (English edition, New Testament Theology, SCM Press, 2012).

12 KH SCHELKLE, *Theologie des Neuen Testaments*, I-IV, Düsseldorf, 1968–1976 (English edition, The Theology of the New Testament, Collegeville, Minnesota, Liturgical Press, 1978).

Testaments. The distinction between biblical theology and dogmatic theology was clear, but the question concerning the limitations of biblical theology as an eminently historical discipline began to be felt. Is it possible for biblical theology to be configured as a neutral discipline limited to investigating the past, while not passing any worthwhile judgement on the texts and the impact they can have on the existential reality of scholars and all their readers? This question expresses well the cultural and religious shift which took place over the last decades of the 20th century. It was a shift which could only but concern biblical research, especially from the point of view of methodological approaches.

The crisis of historico-critical exegesis has highlighted its limitations. Even the results offered thus far by biblical theology, though, have been severely questioned, especially from a methodological point of view. New questions have arisen, and new epistemologies have been proposed. Clearly indicative of this is the study by Leo G. Perdue, *The Collapse of History. Reconstructing Old Testament Theology*,[13] which announced the crisis of an historically-framed biblical theology, which had dominated for decades, and the massive adherence of many scholars to the interpretative criterion proposed already in 1970 by Brevard S. Childs, according to which the canonical nature of the entire Bible is the basis of biblical theology, as shown by the long Christian tradition.[14]

---

13 LG PERDUE, *The Collapse of History. Reconstructing Old Testament Theology*, Minneapolis, 1994, according to which the past that history pretends to recover is, instead, unrecoverable.

14 BS CHILDS, *Biblical Theology in Crisis*, Philadelphia, 1970; ID., *The New Testament as Canon*, Philadelphia, 1985; *Old Testament*

In fact, already since 1961, James Barr had highlighted the distance between the historical events and the accounts the Israelites give of them as God's action in history. They are stories, that is, something approaching history, but they are unable to actually reproduce it. As a consequence, according to Barr it is not God's actions that count but God's word. God speaks more than he acts, and theology should focus on God's discourse, More recently, regarding the Old testament, Walter Brueggemann has insisted on the fact that God is the primary object of theology. Hence, beginning with the analysis of the texts and metaphors that speak of him, what is evidenced is the testimony God gives of himself as mediated through the Torah, the Prophets, other sages, worship,[15] while François Vouga maintains that if the New Testament shows how, from the beginning, the pluralism of interpretation of the Nazrene has been stressed so much, then it means that his message is addressed to every individual and generates an existential relationship which also implies a creative dimension and is therefore open to a multiplicity of interpretations.[16]

In recent decades,, however, approaches have multiplied and, fully reflecting the spirit of the times, a whole range of hermeneutical methodologies has come about, characterized more by the search for theological consistency, out of a

Theology in a Canonical Context, Philadelphia, 1979; *Biblical Theology of the Old and New Testament*, Minneapolis, 1992.

[15] W BRUEGGEMANN, *Theology of the Old Testament. Testimony, Dispute, Advocacy*, Minneapolis, 1997.

[16] F VOUGA, *Une théologie du Nouveau Testament*, Geneva, 2001.

desire to interrelate with other scientific disciplines. Some are of a sociological bent,[17] others are based on rhetorical analysis,[18] some are in strict connection with theologies of liberation[19] and *Black Theology*,[20] while yet others are strongly influenced by feminist critical theory[21] or firmly anchored in the field of *Women's Studies*.[22] We are talking about a change of theological reference models which has momentous importance. It is along this curve that the biblical theology which Bergoglio makes reference to is situated, and is the theological perspective which determines the biblical texture of his preaching and magisterium.

This flourishing of biblical theologies which are not exclusively academic, since they have germinated within a

---

17 J Barr, *The Semantics of Biblical Language*, Oxford, 1961.
18 P Trible, *Rhetorical Criticism. Context, Method, and the Book of Jonah*, Minneapolis, 1994.
19 GV Pixley, *Exodus. A Liberation Perspective*, New York, 1987. Cf. also AF Botta-PA Andiñach (eds), *The Bible and the Hermeneutics of Liberation*, Atlanta, 2009.
20 IJ Mosala, *Biblical Hermeneutics and Black Theology in South Africa*, Grand Rapids, 1989.
21 E Schüssler Fiorenza-M Perroni, 'Lettura femminile ed ermeneutica femminista del NT: status quaestionis', in *Rivista Biblica* 41 (1993), 315–339, 315: 'Una valutazione dell'esegesi femminista: verso un senso critico integrale', in *Studia Patavina* 43 (1996, 67–92; 'L'interpetazione biblica femminista tra ricerca sinnotica ed ermeneutica politica', in *Rivista Biblica* 45 (1997) 439–468.
22 Particularly indicative in this regard is the great series, *The Bible and Women. An Encyclopedia of Exegesis and Cultural History*, which has been published simultaneously in four languages (English, Italian, Spanish, German) and anticipates the publication of twenty volumes covering Old and New Testament from a feminine perspective, a critical reconstruction of twenty centuries of biblical interpretation of women (bibleandwomen.org/EN).

variety of both pastoral and political practices, reminds us that ultimately, it has never been academia which has created the world's reality. Rather has it been an echo of this reality; it has interacted with its learnings and tensions in order to critically develop them, organize them into a collective imagination and make them the object of shared knowledge.

2.2 The new hermenutics

It is precisely within this new epistemological phase that we need to locate a typically Spanish-American theoretical reference model which, since Vatican II, has assimilated some of the features of the theology of liberation and, at the same time, has distanced itself from it to be a 'theology of the people'. Even given its particular character, this model fully reflects the current tendency which is more attentive to the history of the present than merely reconstructing the past, and is dominated by the criterion by which, as far as the Holy Scriptures are concerned, what is of greatest importance is their impact on the various situations characterizing the life of the human community today. Also in theology, by now 'practices' are no longer thought of as an appendix, the mere application of theoretical and abstractly formulated ideas, but are examined as very real *loci theologici*, settings and situations within which even quite different theologies strike root, sprout, and bear fruit.[23]

23 On this, see the *Boston Declaration* marking the first meeting of Iberian and Latin American liberation theologians, men and women, held in the US in February 2017 (https://thebostondeclaration.com/). The question of *loci theologici* would require an entirely different study. In fact, reflection on the

After centuries during which a strongly eurocentric theological model had been exported pretty much everywhere, a model which is rational and ideological in the dogmatic area, and literary-historical in the biblical area, the birth of contextual theologies rooted in local traditions and cultures, contributes to rethinking continuity with the great tradition, dealing with new existential and ethical questions and engaging with new political perspectives.[24] We should be neither surprised nor scandalized by it. For decades, European theology has been modelling itself on philosophical theories that are entirely foreign to

---

relationship between history and theology, other than it having been a constant in the history of theological thinking, can be considered an important indicator of the changes in the theoretical reference horizon. It is enough to recall the Renaissance breakthrough and the first great attempt to systematize theological method by M. Cano, with his concept of history as the last of the ten *loci theologici* from which the theologian can draw certain or only probable arguments "both to corroborate his own opinions and to refute the erroneous opinions of others' (De *locis theologicis* 1,1), to the 19th century awareness of the radical historicity of thought, or the use of the category of the *locus theologicus* by one of the major liberation theologians, Jon Sobrino and the battle he had with the Congregation of the Doctrine of the Faith (Cf. J Costadoat, 'El "lugar teológico" en Jon Sobrino', in *Theologica Xaveriana* 181 [2016], 23–49: http://dx.doi.org/10.11144/javeriana.tx66-181.ltjs).

24 In this respect, a statement of Bergoglio's is absolutely clear: "We are always pursued by the ghost of the Enlightenment, that ideological and nominalist reductionism which leads us not to respect concrete reality." See his preface to the Italian edition of the book by CH Bianchi, *Introduzione alla teologia del popolo. Profilo spirituale e teologico di Rafaele Tello*, EMI, Bologna, 2015, in which Francis once again takes up the presentation he made to the original edition in Buenos Aires, 2013.

the religious thinking of Jesus the Jew or, in deference to emperors and princes, has absorbed the travails of history, claiming to contribute to guiding them: so why should it not do so now at a time when either people hungering for democracy, or women, are emerging on the world scene with increasing force and claiming to be new political subjects?[25] And, as our Western history has widely demonstrated, their being political subjects makes them suitable as hermeneutic subjects.

So, instead of being distinguished for seeking a unifying criterion with which to interpret the many Old Testament and Gospel traditions, the new epistemologies stand out for developing varied biblical theologies characterized by the many kinds of mediations furnished by linguistics and the humanities, especially the social sciences, rather than for identifying a consistent theoretical approach capable of dealing with a hugely diverse collection of biblical traditions and books. Very many hermeneutical possibilities emerge from this which are both rich and attractive at the same time.

We should not forget that, either when the evangelists were searching the Scriptures for criteria and premises on which to develop their theology of Jesus of Nazareth, or

---

25 John XXIII understood this very well when, in the last half of last century, he listed in his Encyclical *Pacem in Terris* (11 April 1963) "women" who are "gaining an increasing awareness of their natural dignity" and "a form of society which is evolving on entirely new social and political lines" because "all over the world men are either the citizens of an independent State, or are shortly to become so", as among the historical processes which should have the value of "signs of the times" for the redeemed (nos 41, 42, 126 ff.).

when various models of biblical hermeneutics or biblical theology have flourished over the long course of the centuries, it is one thing to claim to explain, make sense of the Bible in its every detail, but quite another to make sense of the Bible as such in its totality. In this latter case, the choice of a 'canon within the canon' becomes essential. That is, it becomes necessary to identify some core things within Scripture around which its theological warp and weft can be reconstructed with a degree of coherence. Not all the biblical books have equivalent theological value, nor can individual assertions have such. Ultimately, it is sufficient to think of what Israel did by considering the Pentateuch to be the Torah, the 'canon within the canon' from which to begin interpretation, while also valuing the theology contained in the whole of the Bible. Further on we will see how magisterial documents allow us to identify the 'canon within the canon' from which Francis elaborates his biblical hermeneutics.

First, though, we need to pose the question in line with what has been said thus far: in what sense can one speak of a biblical hermeneutics of Pope Francis? Or, to put in another way: what is the theoretical perspective which acts as the background to his way of not only reading Scripture for personal devotion or edification, but in view of the role of pastor which he must carry out on behalf of a vast community of men and women who believe in Jesus of Nazareth as the one who rose from the dead?

In our view, there are two foundations upon which Francis builds his hermeneutics of the Bible. On the one hand, with the theology of the people as background, his preaching and magisterium have a biblical texture which interweaves kerygmatic purpose with prophetic spirit. On the other, Pope Francis' preaching and magisterium have roots in the precise way of approaching faith which is Ignatian spirituality, and as the first Jesuit pope in history, he cannot, nor does he even want to, give this up.

3. *A kerygmatic purpose and a prophetic vigour*

Very often, especially when commenting on the Sunday Gospel before reciting the *Angelus*, Pope Francis lets us see, even if indirectly, that the great period of historical exegesis did not pass by in vain. He does not employ the abusive approach to texts so dear to ecclesiastical oratory, does not brandish them to find reasons, always and everywhere, to make his listeners feel guilty, nor does he distort these texts while making them useful for his purposes. In a very obviously popular approach, as the situation requires, he aims to pass on the authentic meaning of the Gospel passage, especially if it is about Jesus' teachings. At times, he is less successful when he has to interpret the narrative traditions, because as many still do, Francis, too, yields to the temptation to merely recount the story of all the Gospel accounts, instead of grasping their evocative literary character and strong potential for topical application.

The most typical connotation, though, of Francis' biblical interpretation, as Cardinal Gianfranco Ravasi has rightly noted, comes from his 'conversational' ability, with the meaning that this term has in the New Testament[26] before it

---

26 G Ravasi, 'Una vera "Postfazione". L'omelia secondo Papa

acquired an exclusively liturgical and technical connotation which restricted its meaning to the explanation of the sacred texts within the context of the Eucharistic celebration. The Greek term *homilía* (conversation) and its corresponding verb *homilêin* (to converse), referred to a real-life situation where words are spoken in view of a dialogue. Francis knows that the relationship with the God of the word is a communicative event, which is why his preaching especially, but also his ordinary magisterium, are aimed at establishing contact, starting up a dialogue. They generate the desire to do what the Ethiopian eunuch did in the Acts of the Apostles. He invited Philip to sit next to him in his chariot and help him understand what he was reading (Acts 8:30-32).

For Francis, then, reference to the Bible has a kerygmatic intent above all. It is the meeting ground where the word becomes proclamation, but also challenges, sets up a process which is both exegetic (ἐξήγησις = drawing out), and should guarantee understanding because it draws out the meaningful elements from the Scripture, and hermeneutics (literally, ερμηνευτική = the art of interpretation, translation), which requires the ability to make something understood, because it seeks an explanation of the text, including its potential to speak to the present moment. For Francis, the Bible is prophetic oracle; it involves us, judges and consoles, destroys and builds up.

Pursuing a kerygmatic end with prophetic intent means wanting to encourage a gradual maturing of faith in those

Francesco', in A Cozzi-R Repole-G Piana, *Papa Francesco quale teologia?* Cittadella, Assisi, 2016, 193–208.

who listen, an increasingly aware adherence to the person of Jesus of Nazareth. This is what Francis wants for the Church and for each believer. Knowing all too well that it lies beyond any ecclesiastical strategy, for him the prime level, the deepest one on which the Church's true identity rests, is the constant effort to adhere to what Jesus proclaimed through his life and brought about by his death and resurrection. In strict continuity with early apostolic preaching, and by preaching always, Francis stakes his ministry on proclaiming the gospel *of* Jesus, and proclaiming the gospel *about* Jesus, thus evoking Peter's first declaration at the beginning of his mission: 'I have no silver or gold, but what I have I give you ...' (Acts 3:6). What Francis has to give and does give is his knowledge of the Scriptures which has matured through prayer and the discipline of discernment, but is also rooted in the history of faith of the people.

On the other hand, did not Cardinal Bergoglio speak unequivocally just a few days before his election? He had concluded his brief address to the Congregation of Cardinals which precedes the Conclave (9 March 2013), by offering an identikit of the future pope: 'Thinking about the next pope: a man who, through contemplation of Jesus Christ, and adoration of Jesus Christ, helps the Church go out of itself toward the existential peripheries, helps it to be the fruitful mother who experiences the "delightful and comforting joy of evangelising."' This quotation from Paul VI's 1975 Apostolic Exhortation *Evangelii Nuntiandi* (*EN*) 80, to which Francis has firmly anchored his own Apostolic Exhortation *Evangelii Gaudium* (*EG*), allows us to clearly understand that for him the Petrine ministry finds its principle connotation in evangelization. He wants to call the whole Church to be faithful to what, for him, comes from the apostles, the dissemination of the proclamation about Jesus, as we see from the kerygmatic discourses in Acts,[27] and the proclamation of the salvific value of his death as shown by Paul's apostolic experience.[28]

3.1 A theology 'from the end of the world'

Francis knows very well, then, that indifference to the message of Scripture places the faith at grave risk: various kinds of popular superstition can have strong ascendancy, but believing in the Messiah imposes the effort of a searching faith, a faith which does not conform to the outward appearances of an ordinary, unreflective or indifferent way of life. The message of the Scripture, on the other hand, cannot be reduced to personal, intimate, private internalization. It implies a collective responsibility which each individual takes on at the moment of his or her awareness, in heart and mind, of their personal stance before God and others.

We cannot be surprised, then, if the appeal to Scripture for Francis does not generate either doctrine or devotion but opens up to a 'political' perspective. To come 'from the end of the world' is no mere geographical expression, just as 'the ends of the earth' is not. That is where the Risen Lord sends his disciples 'to be my witnesses in Jerusalem, in all Judea

---

27 Cf. Acts 2:14–39; 3:12–26; 4:10–20; 5:29–32; 10:34–43; 13:16–41; 17:18–31.
28 Cf. 1 Cor 1:23; Gal 1:11–12; Rom 1:3–4.

and Samaria, and to the ends of the earth' (Acts 1:18). How can a man who comes 'from the end of the world' forget that the financial and economic crisis and the dozens of wars plaguing the planet confronts our so-called Christian West with the responsibility of having built up a system by which the rich enjoy themselves at the expense of the poor, and makes the poor pay for the sins of the rich? From a prophetic perspective this mechanism can only appear to go against everything God has said and done, from freeing the Israelites from Egypt to fulfilling the messianic expectation in Jesus of Nazareth (Lk 4:17-21). It is a mechanism which crushes individuals, families, social groups, populations and entire continents, so that economic pressure and the exploitation of earth's goods benefit a minority only and always, and result in arms being the most profitable investment.

If we want to understand the significance of the fact that for the first time ever a pope has been elected who comes 'from the end of the world', and that he wants to reform the Church so it will be 'an evangelizing Church that goes out of itself, the *"Dei Verbum religiose audiens et fideliter proclamans,"'* as he told his brother cardinals, it is then necessary to begin essentially from an understanding of the theology of the people, something we have already hinted at. It is the theological reference model for Bergoglio and also the background to his biblical hermeneutics. This model, too, comes 'from the end of the world,' an expression, along with others, of the fully contemporary situation of a variety of biblical hermeneutics, given the variety of cultures which characterize our time.[29] To put it in Bergoglio's own words, the Latin American continent is 'a continent with many poor people and many Christians.'[30] These words are echoed in the crucial question posed recently by Latin American theologians: 'When is a people Catholic? When it has many churches or when it has little poverty?'[31]

The theology of the people, widely diffused, especially in Argentina, finds its programmatic manifesto in the concluding document of the 5th General Conference of the Latin American and Caribbean Bishops (Aparecida 2007), a notable contributor to which was the then Archbishop Bergoglio.[32] For him, Paul VI's *EN* and the Aparecida Document are the sources from which to essentially draw to achieve an authentic pastoral work of evangelization

---

29 Here we have in mind the illuminating article by Jesuit theologian JC SCANNONE, 'El papa Francisco y la teología del pueblo', in *Razón y Fe*, 1395 (2015), 31–50. This is an important text for understanding not only that Bergoglio is firmly rooted in the theology of the people, but also for articulating the theology of liberation, of which the theology of the people represents a possible version or adaptation.

30 He wrote thus in the preface to the Italian edition of the book by CH BIANCHI, *Introduzione alla teologia del popolo. Profilo spirituale e teologico di Rafael Tello*, Bologna, 2015, in which Francis once again picked up the presentation he had made to the original edition in Buenos Aires in 2012. Rafael Tello is one of the founders of the theology of the people. Suspended *a divinis* and deprived of his teaching role, he was rehabilitated by Bergoglio who has always had words of great respect for him.

31 *Boston Declaration*, 301.

32 See DJ FARES, '10 anni da Aparecida. Alle fonti del pontificato di Francesco', in *La Civiltà Cattolica* 168 (2017 / 4006), 338–352.

and effective inculturation.[33] It is an appeal *ad fontes* which constitutes the fabric of his first Apostolic Exhortation *EG*, the programmatic document of his pontificate.

The 2nd Conference of the Latin American and Caribbean Bishops held at Medellín immediately after the Council,[34] had encouraged the Council's repercussions on one of the 'young Churches' as they were then called, which spread throughout a continent in considerable socio-political but also cultural and ecclesial ferment. Five hundred years were being critically rethought, a long period during which an entire continent had been violated and subjugated amid conquest, colonization and Christianization. It was 1969, and the process of self-determination of peoples was the great challenge which the Churches could no longer avoid. In Argentina, the search for a Church of and for the poor, as Vatican II wanted, had to contend with a very contentious political situation.

Elsewhere, and already for some time in the West, the social sciences were being seen as a privileged partner also of theology, and encouraged the development of new theoretical reference models contrasting with Enlightenment abstraction, which had gone well beyond its intentions to become a solid support for totalitarian regimes

---

33 Nor should we forget that at the Opening Address at the International Conference of Theology, 'Evangelización de la cultura, e inculturación del Evangelio' (1985), Bergoglio had quoted Pedro Arrupe, Superior General of the Jesuits, who had been a pioneer in using the neologism 'inculturation' at the 1974 Synod of Bishops dedicated to *Evangelization in the modern world*.

34 The first was at Rio de Janeiro in 1955.

and ideologies, but also for historiographical positivism. With its presumed neutrality, this latter risked locking historical research into a sterile laboratory. It should not be forgotten that in the 1930s, a French group of scholars from *Les Annales*[35] had brought significant methodological innovations to historiographical research, thanks to a fruitful interdisciplinary exchange with sciences like geography and sociology, and later, economics and other social sciences.

Whoever studied theology in the '70s, could see how fruitful it was to take on epistemological criteria not only from sciences like metaphysical philosophy or philology, but also linguistics or the social sciences, since this encouraged the drawing up of theological models which respected the diversity of cultures.

As regards Church history in particular, it is no longer understood as just the history of popes and councils but as the history of peoples made up of real men and women who in different eras have shaped their faith and belonging to the Church in different ways. It becomes very clear how the new historiographical parameters are fully in line with the understanding which the Council Fathers wanted to impress on the ecclesiological outlook which Vatican II gave the Church in *Lumen Gentium* (*LG*).

3.2 Inculturation of the gospel

Clearly, the category of 'people of God' would find strong echo in cultures such as Latin American ones

---

35 The name of the journal which gave voice to this current of thinking which is called the 'New History'.

who felt that their liberation from years of oppression was strictly connected not only with the struggle against structural injustice and institutionalized violence, but also with the affirmation of their own cultural identity. It is no coincidence that it is not only universities which are considered to be the suitable place for theological discussion and development. In 1966, on return from the Council, the Argentinian bishops established an Episcopal Commission for Pastoral Ministry comprising bishops, theologians, pastoral experts, men and women religious. This became the setting to which the theology of the people owes its genesis. 'People' becomes synonymous with 'the manifold unity of a common culture rooted in a common history aimed at a shared common good.'[36] This is about a prior existing unity in which institutional and structural injustices are understood as betrayal perpetrated against the people by one part of this same people who become an anti-people.

In the theology of the people, then, it is possible to recognize the specific view of the theology of liberation as practised by Argentinian theologians.[37] Already in part of the Puebla Document at the end of the 3rd General Conference of Latina American and Caribbean Bishops (1979), there had been clear recognition of the fact that in Latin America it is the poor who confer a value on the culture of their own people, that structure their lives, and that the option for the poor coincides with the option for

---

36   SCANNONE, 'El papa Francisco', cit. 34.
37   On critiques of this Argentinian line of theology of liberation see *Ibidem*, 37-39.

culture.³⁸ The wisdom of a people who preserve awareness of their roots is not to be thought of as an alternative to scientific culture, which fully retains its complementary value, but encourages mediation between the faith of the people and an inculturated theology.³⁹

This is not the place to subject the category of 'people', quite complex in itself, to careful critical analysis. It is a category, though, that becomes more slippery than ever once theologized as 'people of God', be it in biblical or post-biblical terms, and when it is even sublimated into a 'mystique of the people' – that can end up bordering dangerously on becoming an ideological absolute. However, there is no doubt that European culture is not a little perplexed about the emphasis placed on the category of 'people'. On the one hand there is the searing memory of the enormous price we had to pay a mere few decades ago to free Europe from the sinister and ferocious fantasy of the 'spirit of the people' (*Volksgeist*), and on the other, the complex story of peoples

---

38 It should not be forgotten that the 80s would see hard positions taken by the Congregation for the Doctrine of the Faith against liberation theologians who had adopted class struggle as their hermeneutical principle. See the Instruction *Libertatis Nuntius*, 1984.

39 From a methodological point of view, it entails privileging historico-cultural analysis, albeit without renouncing socio-structural analysis; employing, as tools for understanding reality and transforming it, the more concise and hermeneutical sciences, without rejecting support from the more analytical and structural sciences; anchoring such mediations in an understanding and wise discernment which in turn confirms them; taking a critical distance from the Marxist approach to social analysis, as well as from the cognitive categories and action strategies which derive from it.

who want to redesign the atlas from the point of view of their belief that they are 'the people of God'. This discourse would lead us off-track, even though in reality it would open up an important chapter on *Wirkungsgeschichte*, because it brings with it the question of the relationship between reception of the biblical text and the theology of the Argentinian people.

Perhaps it is still too soon to engage with this problem, so we will limit ourselves to highlighting some connections between the 'theology of the people' and Scripture. A statement by Scannone allows us to make it clear that the relationship between people and religiosity is not to be taken indiscriminately, but must find its key in evangelization, evangelization which activates a hermeneutical circuit of which the people, and therefore the poor, are a first and vital subject. The religion of the people, if authentically evangelized, far from being an opium, has an evangelizing potential, but also potential for human liberation as popular reading of the Bible has in fact shown.[40] We can understand, then, that the people and above all the poor, for Francis, are both evangelized and evangelizers at the same time:[41] 'Once the gospel has been inculturated in a people, in their process of transmitting their culture they also transmit the faith in ever new forms; hence the importance of understanding evangelization as inculturation. Each portion of the people of God, by translating the gift of God into its own life and in accordance with its own genius, bears witness to the faith it has received and enriches it with new and eloquent

---

40 JC Scannone, 'El papa Francisco', cit., 36.

41 This is a somewhat different perspective compared to other kinds of emphasis on religiosity and popular piety like, for

expressions' (*EG*, no. 122). In continuity with the Puebla Document and the one from Aparecida, Francis insists that 'a people continuously evangelizes itself' (*EG*, no. 122).

We need to insist on the fact that in Latin American countries, popular reading of the Bible is a true and proper 'school of exegesis'. It is a collective practice that, as well as fostering evangelization based on the Bible, has been an ecclesial place for reception of the text in view of its inculturation. It has given flesh to Pentecost because it has brought the oracle of the Prophet Joel to fulfilment: 'In the last days it will be, God declares, that *I will pour out my Spirit upon all flesh, and your sons and your daughters shall prophesy, and your young men shall see visions, and your old men shall dream dreams. Even upon my slaves, both men and women, in those days I will pour out my Spirit* and they shall prophesy' (Acts 2:17-18; Joel 3:1-2).

Then, in *EG*, no. 237, Francis himself calls on an important methodological criterion for popular reading of the Bible, that of the 'entire gospel': 'The genius of each people receives in its own way the entire gospel and embodies it in expressions of prayer, fraternity, justice, struggle and celebration … The whole is greater than the part.' That means that it aims at turning itself into the same spirit that animated Jesus' preaching, a prophetic spirit and, as such, one rooted in the biblical tradition. As a good Jew,

---

example, the one proposed by the Italian Episcopal Conference, which does not envisage a robust theological mediation capable of indicating the specific nature of the term 'popular' in a socio-cultural context like that of a post-modern society.

the Prophet of Nazareth knows very well that the part always refers to the whole, and that totality resides not in the quantity received, but in the attitude with which it is received.

It is sufficient to consider the discussion Jesus had with the lawyer who wanted to test him. The 'most important commandment' is not a part of the Law, nor does it exclude the other commandments, but assumes them all at the very moment the hermeneutical criterion is involved. On the other hand, in the logic of the Spirit, the whole is never measured quantitatively, but for the receptive capacity of either the individual or the group: 'with all your heart, with all your soul, with all your strength, and with all your mind' (Lk 10:27, cf. Dt 6:5, Lev 19:18). It is a reception from which none of the dimensions and human potential is excluded. Nor for Francis is it only individuals, because 'The salvation which God has wrought, and the Church joyfully proclaims, is for everyone. God has found a way to unite himself to every human being in every age. He has chosen to call them together as a people and not as isolated individuals. No one is saved by himself or herself individually, or by his or her own efforts. God attracts us by taking into account the complex interweaving of personal relationships in the life of the human community' (*EG*, no. 113).

3.3 A deuteronomic memory

A recent item seems to us to be worthy of much attention. Already, when presenting Ciro Henrique Bianchi's book on the theology of the people,[42] the then Cardinal Bergoglio had made an observation that is worth an entire lesson in biblical theology: 'Popular piety is the cracking open of the memory of a people. It is essentially deuteronomic. We cannot understand it without a deuteronomic framework. And that memory is opened up in different ways.'[43] What does a 'deuteronomic memory' mean? Here, Bergoglio involves the biblical tradition, not just because there is a Book called Deuteronomy in the Bible, but because this book gives testimony to the fact that the strength of Israel's tradition, like that of all traditions, resides in the ability to read the people of God's specific experience from a distance, to interpret it with ever new hermeneutic filters. Deuteronomy, the most ancient core of which goes back to the 8th or 7th century BC and has had various additions to it, rereads and reinterprets the theological motif at the heart of Israel's identity, which is the Covenant relationship God established with his people through the gift of the Law, within the perspective of constant reform, given the many historical events, some strongly destabilizing, which followed.

Since nothing in history remains the same forever, the condition for fidelity is a memory open to taking up what counts from the past and reinterpreting it for an ever new present and an unknown future. This is not about a devout attitude, but a profound sense of belonging to a political

---

42 See above, no. 25
43 See the Italian preface to the book.

history. Far from being a separate history, the history of salvation comes about through this political history. The Bible can be taken as a paradigm of all history: 'With its stories, full of commemorations, the Bible offers us a fundamental pedagogical method: we cannot understand our present time we live in without the past, understood not as a collection of distant facts but as the lifeblood which bathes the present. Without such an awareness, reality loses its unity, history its logical thread, and humankind loses the meaning of its actions and the direction for its future.'[44]

What he did together with his people as bishop, Francis now does together with the entire people of God. For him the 'faithful people' with a deuteronomic memory is today a people made up of peoples, each with its own culture. And the Pope knows very well that the inculturation of the gospel can only take place within each culture. It is no coincidence that Francis placed a sentence by a theologian he has much respect for, Rafael Tello, at the heart of *EG*. Tello rephrases the axiom dear to Scholastic theology, *gratia supponit naturam*, as 'Grace supposes culture, and God's gift becomes flesh in the culture of those who receive it' (EG, no. 115). The nature of each of the earth's peoples coincides, then, with its culture. It is the necessary, unavoidable condition for receiving grace. According to the logic of the Incarnation, it can achieve its most authentic truth and tend to its effective realization only thanks to the proclamation of

---

44 Pope Francis' address to heads of state and governments in the European Union, for the 60th anniversary of the signing of the Treaties of Rome, 25 March 2017.

the gospel of Jesus. Hence, Francis' words and gestures are always understood in a kerygmatic sense.[45]

As a consequence, it is about words and gestures never imprisoned within the rigidity of formal rubrics, making the borders between evangelization, catechesis, teaching, exhortation rigid and insurmountable. With charismatic power, Francis overcomes this kind of specialization in the name of the one ministry of evangelization, of proclamation. Even when he is addressing the whole people of God on the occasion of ordinary magisterium, and doing so with authority, his chief aim is not a cognitive and theoretical teaching, but to transmit a faith which is genetically bound up with its 'practices', first of all prayer and meditation. It is a transmission that seeks to proclaim and persuade, correct and amend. In other words, he wants to educate to justice.

The theology of the people, which even recently Latin American theologians courageously described as a 'propehtic theology which unmasks false gods'[46] and which lies at the basis of his biblical hermeneutics, has taught Francis that a deuteronomic memory, far from being the daughter of melancholy and nostalgia, and even less so of recrimination, is capable of grasping prophecy for the future in the past. This is the biblical hermeneutics that has struck root in the culture of a people which Francis has brought with him from the end of the world.

---

45 It is not just a case of the highly symbolic actions Francis carries out but, as Gianfranco Ravasi rightly notes, of the fact that when he speaks, 'he recovers that important component of language which is its bodiliness' (*Una 'vera' Postfazione*, cit., 195).

46 *Boston Declaration*, cit., 301.

4. Ignatian roots

'I feel that I am a Jesuit in my spirituality; in the spirituality of the *Exercises*, the spirituality I have at heart.' Thus spoke Bergoglio during the press conference held on his return flight from Rio de Janeiro, 28 July, 2013, and much has been written over these four years on the first Jesuit pope in history. No different from other popes who have come from religious life and always stamped their pontificate with salient features of the spiritual tradition they belonged to, Francis too, demonstrates daily that when he was elected pope he did not cease being a Jesuit. On the contrary, he is convinced that for the Church of today so much in need of reform, the Society's charism can be a real *kairos*.

Being a Jesuit means many things, and it is certainly not possible here to pick up all the threads of an identity, a spirituality and a history that has profoundly affected centuries of the Church's life. Francis himself has often woven them together at interviews or during meetings with his confreres. What interests us here is a quite particular detail, namely, the influence of Ignatian spirituality on his biblical hermeneutics. There is no question that it has strongly influenced the theology of the people, given the fact, too, that a good number of Jesuits played a part in its birth and growth, and also given the significant contribution made by Jorge Mario Bergoglio in the drafting of the Aparecida Document as president of the Editorial Commission for the final document.

4.1 The spirituality of the *Exercises*

At the roots of the identity of the Society of Jesus lie the *Spiritual Exercises* (*SE*) which Ignatius of Loyola wrote between 1522 and 1535, and which were approved by Paul III in 1548. They can be truly considered to be the trademark of the Society and of every individual Jesuit. What seems especially useful to us to observe here, is that with the drawing up of the *SE*, Ignatius realized a very real work of inculturation of the gospel.

To understand the importance of this, however, we need to begin with his conversion experience. It is tied to a place, Montserrat, the Benedictine monastery in Catalonia, where spiritual fervour was great and where Ignatius confirmed the life-changing decision that had matured during his pilgrim journey. It was a powerful experience, culminating in confession and the vigil before the image of the Black Madonna, after which Ignatius removed his military and pilgrim gear, thus symbolically leaving his past behind.[47] This bit of history is well known. Less well known, though, are the other stages in the process of writing the *SE*.

According to the monumental biography by the first secretary of the Society, Juan Alfonso de Polanco, it was Ignatius himself, in a 1552 circular, who said something that had not previously been revealed regarding the *SE* and the novelty of the Society: 'A novelty of religion, yes, even if of

---

[47] For reports on Ignatius at Montserrat, you can look at Dom A Albareda, *Sant Ignasi a Monserrat*, ediciò a cura de Josep M. Soler i Canals, Publicacions de l'Albadia de Montserrat, Montserrat 1990.

means ordinarily used among others, especially the spiritual exercises, *or to put it better*, [they are] novel in the practice and manner of doing them (which is new, not the exercises themselves).'[48] In the *SE* which Ignatius wrote, then, the novelty does not lie so much in the exercises themselves but in the 'practice and manner of doing them.' There is a question of something more than simply method. As we will see, the real revolution in perspective wrought by Ignatius lies here.

During his stay at Montserrat, Ignatius came to know Dom Jean Chanones, '*vir prudens, doctus et pius*,' who prepared him for his spiritual confession, one that would take three days.[49] Through Chanones, Ignatius came into contact with the book *Exercitatorium spirituale*, which the great Abbot of Montserrat, García Jiménez de Cisneros, promoter of monastic, ecclesiastical and cultural reform in Spain during the time of the Catholic kings, had written for the spiritual reform of the monks of the Order of St Benedict.[50] Printed in 15000, the *Exercitatorium* is among the books which spread the *devotio moderna* movement

48 P DE LETURIA, 'Génesis de le ejercicios de S. Ignacio y su influjo en la fundación de la Compañía de Jesús (1521-1540)', in *Estudios Ignacianos*, II, Rome, 1957, 3-58 (cit. in ALBAREDA, *Sant Ignasi a Montserrat*, VIII).

49 In this regard, see R GARCÍA VILLOSLADA, *Sant'Ignazio di Loyola. Una nuova biografia*, San Paolo, Cinisella Balsamo, 1997.

50 '*Igitur importuna instantia quorundam nostrorum Fratrum et non improbae temeraritas audacia me induxit, ut de Exercitiis spiritualibus aliquam facere compilationem*': RP GARCÍA CISNERIO, *Exercitatorium spirituale*, Praefatio autoris, editio nova, Ratisbonae, MDCCCLVI.

throughout Spain, born in Holland already by the end of the 14th century, and it had come out of the strong desire for reform which in many ways shook up all of Christianity between the end of the Middle Ages and the beginning of modernity. His was a point of no return. It triggered a creative process in him which would lead him to conceive of a new paradigm of spiritual and ecclesial life capable of expressing the spirit of the times, and was above all a new form of inculturation of the gospel. The Church emerged from the Middle ages with difficulty, and lagging seriously behind the great transformations taking place. Other than the map of the world being altered, political systems and cultural horizons, social organization and individual identities were being modified. Whatever institution there was, was in need of reform, but it was individuals, no longer groups, who dominated the scene. Like Luther, Ignatius too, postulated radical reform, but by contrast with Luther, his reform was about individuals, not structures. It was a reform that would enable people to stay within the history of their time, living fully amid the changes, indeed transforming them into new challenges for spreading the gospel. Ignatius' shift from Abbot Cisneros' *Execitatorium* to the *SE* attests to the shift from a spirituality rooted in the monastic *stabilitatis loci* and a mission approach aimed essentially at the founding of new monasteries, to a spirituality by now clearly shaped by the missionary adventure understood as obedience to the Roman Pontiff *circa missiones*. Ultimately, it was what Francis has us understand when he never tires of repeating that time is greater than space.

It is Pope Francis himself who has let us understand what all this means, with an apparently marginal comment. In the first part of the lengthy interview granted him in August 2013,[51] the editor of *La Civiltà Cattolica*, Antonio Spadaro, asked the Pope to outline his spiritual biography. No surprise that it is strongly marked by his choice to enter the Society, but it cannot be left unobserved that the Jesuit Bergoglio took advantage of the opportunity to make an important clarification: 'Ignatius is a mystic, not an ascetic ... [An interpretation of the *SE*] that emphasizes asceticism, silence and penance is a distorted one that became widespread even in the Society, especially in the Society of Jesus in Spain. Instead, I am rather close to the mystical movement.' Thus he places himself in strict continuity with other great Jesuit theologians of last century, like Karl Rahner and Michel de Certeau.

From ascesis to mysticism: here is Ignatius' creative impulse. By contrast with Abbot Cisneros, for him the *SE* are not a practice aimed at reforming monastic life, and therefore ascetic by prevalence. Nor do they respond to the need to conform to the life of a cenobitic community. This is what lies behind the original wisdom of the Rule of St Benedict. A child of his time and history, Ignatius makes a demanding pedagogy of the *SE* for 'preparing and disposing the soul to rid itself of all inordinate attachments and, after

---

51 A. Spadaro, Interview with Pope Francis, https://w2.vatican.va/content/francesco/en/speeches/2013/september/documents/papa-francesco_20130921_intervista-spadaro.htm

their removal, of seeking and finding the will of God in the disposition of our life for the salvation of our soul.'[52]

For the man who was beginning to take his first steps into modernity, the will of *'Deus semper maior'*, which is at the heart of the entire journey of the *SE*, is no longer measured only on the basis of the individual's salvation, and it is not achieved through ascesis, but by now it is addressed to the salvation of everyone in the world. The boundaries of this world are constantly extended, but have become much more attainable.

Just as in the weeks established by Abbot Cisneros, also in Ignatius' four week programme the meditation topics are distributed in orderly fashion, beginning with a purgative way (*deformata reformare*) to arrive at a unitive way (*conformata confirmare* and *confirmata transformare*). But in the *SE*, Ignatius is tackling more of a linear than a circular process, more aimed at the future, open to the new rather than being addressed to renewed fidelity to the ancient Rule. Shot through with a strong mystical tension of conformation to Christ, culminating in the 'third degree of humility,'[53] as well as 'thinking with the Church,'[54] it opens

---

52 This is the first of the observations [annotations] 'to give some idea of the *Spiritual exercise*', with which Ignatius begins the text of the *SE*.

53 'In order to imitate and be in reality more like Christ our Lord, I desire and choose poverty with Christ poor, rather than riches; insults with Christ loaded with them, rather than honours; I desire to be accounted as worthless and a fool for Christ, rather than to be esteemed as wise and prudent in this world' (ES 167).

54 See the eighteen rules Ignatius puts at the end of the *Exercises* for 'the true attitude of mind we ought to have in the

up to the mysticism of mission, as would become explicit in the contemplation of the two standards (*SE* 137-147) and programmatic in the *Formula* on which the Order was established.[55] It is a mysticism in which the affections, once purified, achieve the full and complete freedom to place themselves at the disposal of the eternal and universal King.

Hence, Francis recognizes himself very much in Peter Faber, Ignatius' first companion, who shared not only his studies with him, but also the intense capacity to 'feel and relish things inwardly.' This was a decisive capacity for the genuine success of the *SE*. Already in the second observation, Ignatius warned how important it was for the person giving the *SE* to help the exercitants discover things through their own reasoning and intellect, because this gives 'greater spiritual relish' (*SE* 3).[56] Ultimately, the Ignatian *SE* only wants to provide cues, ordered and consistent of course, but what is important is that the person making the *Exercises* feels called to bring all his or her dimensions of being to them: freedom, memory, intellect, will as expressed in the prayer '*Take, Lord, and receive*' at the end of the contemplation of the first point on attaining the love of God.[57]

---

church militant' (*SE* 352-370)

55 'to fight under the sacred banner of the Cross, and to serve only God and the Roman pontiff' (*Formula 1*)

56 In order to understand this early Jesuit more closely, cf. A SPADARO, *Pietro Favre, Servitore della consolazione*. Ancora, 2014.

57 'Take, Lord, and receive all my liberty, my memory, my understanding, and my entire will, all that I have and possess. Thou hast given all to me. To Thee, O Lord, I return it. All is Thine,

A few months after his election, Francis sought for Peter Faber to be canonized, because only the dream of a mystic, of someone whose heart is able to combine ideas and reality, flies high. The strength of this 'reformed priest', as he has been called, lay in his conviction that when one learns to converse with God with all the energy of one's feelings and affections, one also becomes capable of taking the most demanding decisions.

How does all this leave a clear mark on Pope Francis' biblical hermeneutics? From a general point of view, there is no doubt that his christological, ecclesial and missionary spirituality has a strong dimension of martyrdom to it. Francis himself recalled this when he celebrated the bicentenary of the restoration of the Society: 'Let us remember our history: He has graciously granted the Society "the privilege not only of believing in Christ, but of suffering for him as well" (Phil 1:29). It does us well to remember this.'[58] When Francis reminds his confreres that the grace of martyrdom is part of the very makeup of the Society, he is calling to mind this fundamental law which has stained its entire history with blood and become a kind of 'deuteronomic' memory for Jesuits.

Without going into detail, some general observations on the contemplations Ignatius proposes for the second, third and fourth weeks of the *SE*, without them claiming in any way to be a form of exegesis, are the result of the Gospel

dispose of it wholly according to Thy will. Give me Thy love and Thy grace, for this is sufficient for me.' (*SE* 234).

58 Homily at solemn Vespers, 27 September, 2014.

texts, and allow us to focus on the biblical hermeneutics which pervades the *SE*.

Whoever makes the *SE*, we said, is called to enter into the dynamics of the *Exercises* with their whole being. Purified by the corrective path taken in the first week, in the weeks that follow, the exercitant is then able to apply the senses to each of the episodes indicated: the flight into Egypt (*SE* 132 or 169), or, over two days, the whole of the passion account (*SE* 209), or one of the mysteries from the Resurrection to the Ascension (*SE* 226). It is a kind of *mise en scène* which makes people more than spectators. It is clearly similar to the attitude required of the observant Jew, to love God 'with all your heart, and with all your soul, and with all your strength and with all your mind' (Lk 10:27; cf. Dt 6:5; Lev 19:18), especially in terms of a time in history strongly marked by attention to the individual subject.

It is also interesting to note that the use of the imagination, while not drawing a strictly faithful account from the Gospel text, does have its own rigour, because it helps to define the context and suggest analogies, two procedures which aim at involving the reader in the account in the former case, and in its meaning, in the latter.

The context suggested for the contemplation, including outside the four weeks, involves 'the mysteries of the life of Our Lord Jesus Christ' presented summarily (*SE* 262-312), prefaced by a significant note from a methodological point of view (*SE* 261: 'all the words that are in quotation marks are from the Gospel itself, but not those that are outside the quotation marks'), because it indicates considerable respect for the biblical text.

Finally, one last observation allows us to outline a kind of Ignatian biblical hermeneutics pervading the whole text of the *SE*. The succession of contemplations distributed over three weeks, from the Incarnation to the Resurrection, is firmly set within a double frame which confers a precise orientation on the whole. Ignatius proposes beginning the second week with an extremely important exercise and invents the parable of the two kings, the purpose of which is to provide the correct key for interpretation of the contemplation that follows on the mysteries of the *life of Christ*. The parable is about the call and mission, and aims at specifying the purpose and meaning of the Incarnation. So, the mysteries of Christ's life do not begin from Bethlehem: the entire Christology of the *SE* is focused on Christ the preacher, on his tireless mission of proclamation which we are invited to associate ourselves with. On the other hand, the Christ who calls us to share the ministry of evangelization with him, is the Christ who is risen and seated at the right hand of the Father, the eternal Lord. In turn, then, Ignatius' Christology moves within the fulfilment of the Father's will, and hence of the grand economy of salvation of the entire universe (*SE* 95).

These are some of the observations that can be made on the relationship between Ignatius' *SE* and the Bible. It is about method more than content, given that the *devotio moderna* is focused on the life and *imitatio Christi* and, at a time when the Bible was found more and more on the fringes of the Catholic Faith, the different spiritual currents did not flourish within the texts of either the Old or New Testament.

Our reception of Francis and his magisterium struggles between the categories of modernism and anti-modernism. It is certainly right as well as inevitable, given the climate in which he is exercising his ministry and the precise choices made so far. But Francis is first of all a true son of Ignatius, that is, of an incipient and dominant modernity in which the centrality of the subject is a powerful resource.

On the other hand, the importance given to method is another of the strong connotations of Ignatian spirituality which Pope Francis firmly stamped on both the planning for and discussion at the Synod on the Family, which involved the whole Church for a good two years. Francis demonstrated his willingness there to fully apply Ignatian pedagogy, which in turn has been imbued with the spirituality of the *SE*.

4.2 The pedagogical method of the *Ratio Studiorum*

It is not possible here to dwell at length on the *Ratio Studiorum* (*RS*), the collection of rules ultimately formulated in 1599 when Sabino Acquaviva was Superior General, but the *RS* has strongly influenced the birth of the modern school.[59]

From then on the *Ratio* has guided Jesuit pedagogical and scholastic activity, and set in motion the long process

---

59 This is not about a desk-bound set of rules. The *Ratio* has a twofold experience behind it. On the one hand that of the Parisian university model from which Ignatius and some of his first companions had learned to consider learning as a process, and, as a consequence, to mark its gradualness. On the other hand it was the experience the Jesuits had already acquired, given that in just a few decades, the Society's involvement in instruction and education

which led schools in Europe to more clearly determine their educational purpose and the learning approaches essential for pursuing it.[60] We are at least interested in highlighting how much the *RS* has influenced Francis' biblical hermeneutics, given that it translates the guiding principle on *non multa sed multum*[61] of Ignatian spirituality into a methodological set of rules useful in the formation of the individual through learning.

Although the *RS* posits Thomist philosophy as the basis for learning, there is no lack of openings toward authors interested in questions regarding Scripture, as well as the Fathers, Councils, papal documents and Church history, in the effort to reach a synthesis of positive Doctors of the Church (Augustine, Jerome …) able to move people emotionally, and Scholastic Doctors (Aquinas, Bonaventure …) able to define and explain. Ignatius recommended this among his rules for thinking with the Church (*SE* 363), but the pedagogical method of the *RS* makes it explicit and directs it strongly to the defence of the Catholic Faith. It nurtures this thanks to constant exercises of *repetitio* and regular practical classes, contexts and debates.

It is worth picking out one aspect of the *RS* here which is very much evident in the daily preaching Francis has engaged in from the day of his election, as an essential expression

---

had led to many schools coming into being throughout the world.

60 When the Society was re-established after being dissolved in the 18th century, a new *Ratio* was promulgated in 1832, then undergoing further revision in the 20th century.

61 According to the second of the Observations at the beginning of the *SE*.

of the Petrine ministry. Motivation plays a large role in the Jesuit scholastic approach and, as a consequence, recognition of the great value emotional aspects play in the cognitive process, even before informative content, or in other words, awareness of the emotions bound up with both the object of study and the strictly individual meanings connected with the aims of learning. The *non multa sed multum* rule, then, comes home to its original setting, that of learning,[62] and to the importance of strategies for internalizing what is learned. The ways matters are approached become more important than their content.

Hence, the vigour of Francis' preaching lies in his ability to transmit the gospel *sine glossa*, always encouraging a deep perception of what has been proclaimed, and thus calling on the imagination, application of the senses and an overall view, memory and interpretation. Proclamation of the gospel is meant to translate into a choice for the gospel. We will have a chance to examine this more thoroughly in what follows.

5. *Reception of the Council*

There is no doubt that Francis' biblical hermeneutics, which places the *kerygma* of salvation at the centre and is strongly marked by its prophetic vigour, must also be understood in connection with the Second Vatican Council.

---

62 This is a proverb dear to the Roman world, as shown by Pliny the Younger (*Epistolae 7,9*) and Quintilian (*Institutiones* 10, 1, 59), but also found in a fragment of Heraclitus in which he maintained that true culture is based on quality and deepening rather than abundance of content.

Bergoglio did not take part in it, but seeing the choices which have marked the first years of his pontificate, he has certainly internalized its spirit and teaching. On the other hand, it is precisely this that has been the cause of angry reactions to him: his pontificate reopens a discussion which many were hoping had been interrupted once and for all.

Francis knows all too well that elements of continuity with the past can never prevent the ferment of discontinuity which prepares for the future, so he does not allow himself to become entangled in the contrast between the hermeneutics of continuity and discontinuity. Instead, he situates himself within the complex course of reception of Vatican II, of the unachieved expectations, ambiguous words, eloquent silences, choices made by some, the acquiescence of many, and tries to retie the threads of that event which still has so much to say to the Church. For sure, one of those threads is the Church's obedience to the Word. As we have recalled, he had already told the Congregation of Cardinals prior to the Conclave, that the Church was in need of reform, to be an 'evangelizing Church that goes out of itself, the "*Dei Verbum religiose audiens et fideliter proclamans!*"'

It also seems possible, although Francis has never explicitly alluded to it, that we can link his reception of the Council to an event which marked the end of the Council, the Pact of the Catacombs with which a number of bishops from around the world, including some from Latin America, sought to seal the beginning of their acceptance of the spirit and letter of that great ecclesial event that would come to a close a few days later. If we read the text of that Pact today,[63] we are struck by the new horizon Francis has begun to draw since the outset of his ministry. It is in harmony with that text, and shows that something which took place on the sidelines fifty years or more ago, carried instead a seed of the future within it.

In fact, at the Council, a century's rift between the Church and the poor had then shown up in all its clarity, and in this respect the Pact of the Catacombs marked a turning point, because it expressed a precise willingness for serious conversion of mind and habits. As stated in the introductory lines: 'We bishops assembled in the Second Vatican Council, are conscious of the deficiencies of our lifestyle in terms of evangelical poverty ...' A clear signal that finally, churchmen wanted their life and choices to be inspired by the gospel, lay in the fact that for each of the twelve points articulated in the Pact, references were to New Testament texts alone.

These forty-two bishops who met at the Catacombs of Saint Domitilla to celebrate the Eucharist and sign the Pact, and the five hundred bishops who signed up later, had understood from their own experience of the Council that the desired *aggiornamento* (updating) of the Church would happen only with a courageous comparison with the letter of the gospel, and the preferential option for the poor.

Whoever reads the Pact of the Catacombs today has the clear impression that Jorge Mario Bergoglio had embodied

---

63   There is an entire website now dedicated to it: https://www.pactofthecatacombs.com/

it as Archbishop of Buenos Aires, and embodies it today as Bishop of Rome. It is a direct summons to the bishops, their attitudes and daily performance, their way of living, dressing, the risk of giving in to vanity and being tempted by power, and it commits them to taking clear positions on behalf of justice, and to putting pressure on international organizations to adopt 'economic and cultural structures which, instead of producing poor nations in an ever richer world, make it possible for the poor majorities to free themselves from their wretchedness.' It had to be clear that, as Francis so often repeats, 'the preferential option for the poor' did not mean recognizing that the Church has financial and economic skills that lie outside its nature and purpose, but that it could, and indeed must, testify to the fact of a fully possible change in the lifestyle of its pastors. The bishops, in the first instance, committed themselves to being a visible testimony to the 'poor Church for the poor' which the Council wanted.

Pervading the Pact of the Catacombs is that 'smell of the sheep' proposed by Francis at the beginning of his pontificate as the measure of the Church's pastoral ministry; the smell of the sheep which is the smell of the gospel. Those who signed the Pact of the Catacombs had claimed they would translate it into a lifestyle worthy of pastors, but possibly because of this, their voice became weaker as the days went by, their presence more marginal, until death ratified their removal from the ecclesial scene and historical memory – at least until the election of Jorge Mario Bergoglio.

6. *The service of the Word*

For Francis, service of the Word and service to the poor are inseparable. He is fully in tune with the dictates of the New Testament. One of the many misunderstandings that weighs upon the theological understanding of ministry in the Latin Church, comes from an interpretation of the account at the beginning of the Acts of the Apostles regarding the conflict which arose in the Jerusalem community (Acts 6:1-6), and which impacted on Church structures to follow. The text was used in an overly simplistic way as the foundation for the ministry of the diaconate, people responsible for charitable work distinct from the apostles who had 'the service of the Word' as their task. The connection between charity and the Word is really less schematic. Read in context, the excerpt does not permit the separation of two different functions. Rather does it testify to the fact that from the beginning, the community of believers in the Risen Lord had founded their life on the service of the Word and the service of charity, both of which services were carried out either by the group of Twelve for the Judaeo-Christians in Jerusalem, or by the group of Seven for the Judaeo-Christians of the diaspora. In fact, it would be thanks to the evangelizing mission of the Seven that the gospel would go out from Palestine, and that the great mission to the Gentiles would begin. Without wanting to downplay the need which came about with the passing of time, we must however recognize that the text of Acts posits the twin service as the basis of the ecclesial community's life: the Word and charity. And it is precisely in this twin 'diakonia' that Francis' ministry finds its roots.

The Apostolic Exhortation *EG*, which he himself asks us to refer to as the manifesto of his pontificate,[64] is a far-reaching document that cannot be treated summarily. Just as the circulation of the blood in a living being can only be examined in its regular, silent, vital flow, so must this document be read, savoured and assimilated in its every point and as a whole. For Francis, *EG* is 'his synthesis', and as he says himself, 'where your synthesis is, there lies your heart' (*EG*, no. 143). Clearly, here we can only suggest some rapid considerations on the way in which Francis exercises his service of the Word, taking into account one aspect in particular, preaching. Ultimately, it is revealing of his biblical hermeneutics.

One observation, first of all, seems decisive: preaching, for Francis, even of the informal kind, and thus occurring 'in any place: on the street, in a city square, during work, on a journey' (*EG*, no. 127), can imply, inasmuch as it is a proclamation to culture, 'proclaiming the gospel message to ... professional, scientific and academic circles' (*EG*, no. 132), or it can occur in a precise formal context such as the liturgy, where we need not think it must always be communicated by 'fixed formulation learned by heart or by specific words which express an absolutely invariable content' (*EG*, no. 129). In fact, preaching means proposing a hermeneutics of

---

64   'Allow me to leave you just one indication for the coming years: in every community, in every parish and institution, in every diocese and circumscription, in every region, try to launch, in a synodal fashion, a deep reflection on *Evangelii Gaudium*...' (Address to the Fifth Convention of the Italian Church, Florence, November 2015).

gospel proclamation capable of encouraging its embodiment in a culture.

On this point too, Francis is perfectly consistent with his theological model. For him, the gospel needs to be 'preached in categories proper to each culture', because that way it will 'create a new synthesis with that particular culture' (*EG*, no. 129). As we said earlier, it is about a theology of the people which cannot be based on the crystallization of God's Revelation in abstract formulas that never vary, but is realized within a slow, lengthy process. It requires a Church that does not let itself be paralyzed by fear, which results in it looking on while it stagnates (*EG*, no. 129).

It is not difficult to perceive the profound affinity that exists between Francis' biblical hermenuetics and the different theologies of each of the biblical books, but especially to grasp how much his theological reference model reflects the profound theological dynamic that makes the Bible multifaceted but at the same time a unified whole. Just as the theology of each biblical book expresses a precise point of synthesis, and thus manifests one of the many different ways the encounter between God and the individual has taken place, between God and the people he chose, and between God and human beings, so for Francis, reference to a Scripture which never ceases to be a spoken word, generates a dialogue that is 'much more than the communication of a truth' (*EG*, no. 142), because it aims at a synthesis between message and culture, or in other words, between those who dialogue. Hence, as we were saying, for him 'where your synthesis is, there lies your heart' (*EG*, no. 143).

It is impossible to explain in just a few lines his tireless preaching weekdays and Sundays, by examining the content of his various homilies. They need to be heard or read, sure, but also meditated upon rather than being commented upon. Yet without getting into this, it is possible to make some observations on method. Francis himself heads us in this direction by dedicating a good twenty-four paragraphs of *EG* (nos 135–159) to the homily.

For him, 'the homily is the touchstone for judging the pastor's closeness and ability to communicate to his people' (*EG*, no. 135). This is precisely why it has become a stumbling block. Francis knows this well, and is not afraid to denounce it when he says that 'the faithful attach great importance to it,' and he knows that 'both they and their ordained ministers suffer because of homilies: the laity from having to listen to them and the clergy from having to preach them!' (*EG*, no. 135). Or when he reminds us that preparation for preaching requires the ability to give it 'a prolonged time of study, prayer, reflection and pastoral creativity' (*EG*, no. 145).

If, on the one hand, the homily as part of the liturgical context should guide 'the assembly, and the preacher, to a life-changing communion with Christ in the Eucharist' (*EG*, no. 138), on the other, it needs to be spoken 'in our mother tongue,' thus finding 'in the heart of the people and their culture a source of living water, which helps the preacher to know what must be said and how to say it' (*EG*, no. 139). The danger of a purely moralistic or doctrinaire preaching, or one which turns into a lecture on biblical exegesis, impoverishes the quasi-sacramental character of a communication which, as St Paul says in his Letter to Christians in Rome, comes from hearing the word of Christ (Rom 10:17), and from a dialogue 'which is much more than the communication of a truth' (*EG*, no. 142). 'The challenge of an inculturated preaching consists in proclaiming a synthesis, not ideas or detached values' (*EG*, no. 143).

One colleague, a liturgist, asked himself somewhat quizzically whether or not Francis had a liturgical sense. The facts speak for themselves: during one of his Eucharistic celebrations, in a packed square, the people listen and recollect in prayerful silence. Even though it is common knowledge that during their formation Jesuits do not pay special attention to the liturgy, Pope Francis' *ars celebrandi*, strongly focused on the authenticity of his word and the intensity of his gestures, is a clear and strong expression of his *diakonia*, his service of the Word. His word as preacher, which never takes too long, ensures that the Lord, more than his minister, is the centre of attention.

***

What we have said thus far now allows us to get to the heart of the different documents to which Francis has entrusted the diffusion of his magisterial guidance. Without claiming to weigh up each of the individual statements, we would like to focus on their biblical fabric.

Chapter 2
GAUDIUM, LAUS, LAETITIA, MISERICORDIA

As we have seen, the history of biblical interpretation has always been, and always will be articulated by a whole range of interpretative paradigms. Born of history, the Bible reflects all of its contradictions, and is thus a collection of books which is anything but linear and uniform. While exegesis makes an effort not to overlook any of the biblical passages, and tries to interpret them in their literary context, submitting them to literary and historical criticism, biblical theology and biblical hermeneutics, instead, must proceed by constructing interpretative models able to identify and explain the meaning of the biblical message overall.

1. A canon within the canon

To construct an interpretative model of Scripture, every biblical theology and biblical hermeneutics relies on a 'canon within the canon': one or more theological threads among those we find in the Bible – and therefore, some biblical texts which express the direction they take in a particularly eloquent way – are brought together in an interpretative paradigm from which we can trace and draw out the biblical message as a whole.

It is true that this could lead to any hermeneutics being accused of bias, but it is actually this which gives it not only its effectiveness, but its very methodological correctness.

Liberation and feminist theologies especially have helped formalize with extreme clarity the need to establish a perspective to start from, which enables us to grasp the meaning of the whole biblical revelation, and have identified it in God's explicit will to come to the aid of his people, as is already shown at the beginning of the Book of Exodus, and then throughout the prophetic tradition until the proclamation of Jesus of Nazareth.

On the other hand, the Bible is a great mixture of texts that refer to an endless array of situations, and which transmit an endless array of narratives suggesting endless ways of living. Ultimately, the Roman Catholic Church preferred, for a good four centuries, to reiterate the ban on free reading of the Bible by the faithful, also because, given its strong internal contradictions and some parts which are difficult to accept as an expression of the thinking of a good and just God, it is and remains a collection of texts which are not always easy to interpret. The increasingly head-on confrontation with Protestants who, by contrast, considered the Scripture to be the basis of preaching and the obedience of faith, then further hardened Catholic prejudice, and up until the Second Vatican Council, the Bible had been sidelines if not exiled even, from the life of the Catholic Church.[1] On the other hand, the influence on Catholic theology of nineteenth century rationalism with

---

1 The question of the relationship between Churches, theologies and the Bible, is much more articulated and complex than this simple schematization: in this regard, see A AUTIERO-M PERRONI (eds), *La Bibbia neela storai d'Europa. Dalle divisioni all'incontro*, Dehoniane, Bologna, 2012.

its insistence on developing doctrinal, abstract statements, and therefore ones devoid of contradictions and clashes of principle, made it even more unrelated to and distant from botht he theologies of the various biblical books and a theology of revelation able to explain the relationship between faith and history.

In fact, the tension between exegesis and biblical theology on the one hand, and systematic theology on the other, is still a hot issue, and in order not to fall into the trap of direct opposition, many biblical scholars and theologians begin to sense the effectiveness of reference to methodological contributions borrowed from the human sciences. In the first instance, we have already indicated this from history understood as social history, and from sociology. This means that both theologians and biblical scholars recognise in hermmeneutics a good antidote to the risk of doctrinaire fundamentalism for the former, and of literalism for the latter. It seems completely clear that the assertion of truth cannot, nor must not occur at the expense of reality. The 'too bad about the facts' approach of Hegelian memory is finally dismissed as the expression of past thinking, and no longer brandished as a universal principle of interpretation.[2]

From this perspective, the theology of the people which matured within the Argentinian Church is an experiment of great interest, especially at a time when Bergoglio suggests it as a possible reference model for the entire Church. What does it mean and what does it entail for the Universal

---

2   Masterful in this regard is Francis' reflection in nos 231–233 of *Evangelii Gaudium*.

Church that 'the people' are the hermeneutical criterion for interpreting and changing history and that within it, the first incumbents of its deepest and most authentic identity are the poor? We expressed some doubts earlier in this regard which come, in all likelihood, from a comparison between cultural and theological traditions which are different. Perhaps we still need time to evaluate fully the significance of moving on from euro-centrism, of the contribution of post-colonial theologies, of the value of the conflict between or the intertwining of hermenutical models, even those profoundly different from one another. Whoever knows a little bit of Church history or the history of theology, knows that nothing of doctrine or discipline has been completely unchangeable, and that the strength of the tradition lies precisely in the variety of interpretative paradigms of reality, and in the dialectic between the centre and the peripheries.

But today, the rules of this dialectic have radically changed, because there is no longer only one centre, but especially because even in a strongly centralized institution like the Catholic Church, it is the centre itself which has changed, given that it is no longer an Italian or European pope who is carrying out the Petrine ministry, but an Argentinian one. We see how difficult it is, furthermore, to accustom ourselves to the variety of hermeneutical models, and how harking back to the past betrays the belief that a European hermeneutics or a universal one, while being rooted in the culture of other peoples, can only be biased.

Before pausing to consider each of the four magisterial documents thus far published, it still seems important to us to introduce a brief overall consideration. From their titles it becomes quite clear what Francis' 'canon within the canon' is. A title can never be casually chosen. As well as summing up the entire document, it must reflect its purpose, and at the same time allow us to perceive the theological perspective within which the author is developing his thinking. *Gaudium, laus, laetitia, misericordia*: four terms with a strong biblical connotation, shrewdly chosen to highlight the tradition of promise which has opened up through the prophetic tradition, to messianic expectation, and, thanks to its fulfilment in Jesus of Nazareth, becomes a proclamation of joy for all the peoples.

The *leitmotiv* of Francis' biblical hermeneutics, then, insists on a trusting attitude, acknowledgement of God's presence in history, and gratitude because this presence is benevolent and full of grace. Joy, praise, happiness, mercy are the registers on which is modulated the biblical theology of a pope who has learned from Ignatian spirituality 'to call to mind the special favour I have received ... ponder with great affection how much God our Lord has done for me, and how much he has given me of what he possesses; ... and consider, according to all reason and justice, what I ought to offer the Divine Majesty, that is, all I possess and myself with it. Thus as one would do who is moved by a great feeling' (*SE* 234).

2. *Evangelii Gaudium*'s hymn to joy

An eternally new source of joy: for Pope Francis, this is the Scriptures which the Jewish and Christian tradition have preserved and passed on from generation to generation.

For him, Scripture is able to transform those who accept its message, can give meaning to their existence, and guide human coexistence toward forms of fairness and justice. It is no coincidence, then, that *Evangelii Gaudium* (EG), his first Apostolic Exhortation written a few months after his election to publicize the guidelines for his pontificate, is like a large fresco whose colourful harmonies are guaranteed by continuous cross-reference to the biblical roots of faith.

The reasoning is logical, coherent, and develops within a variety of subjects: from the missionary constitution of the Church (*EG*, nos 20–49), to its capacity for gospel disscernment in order to recognise and tackle the challenges coming from today's world, and the need for the Church's missionary renewal (*EG*, nos 50–109); from the kerygmatic direction to be impressed on all pastoral activity (*EG*, nos 110–175) to the social dimension of evangelization (*EG*, nos 176–258). It never delves into theological speculation, because 'ideas disconnected from realities give rise to ineffectual forms of idealism and nominalism, capable at most of classifying and defining, but certainly not calling to action' (*EG*, no. 232), nor is it concerned with refuting and condemning doctrinal errors. Francis does not yield to facile kinds of irenicism or mere sociological approaches, because the basic criterion of his discernment, that 'realities are greater than ideas' is fully theological, deeply rooted in the incarnation of the word and its being put into practice: 'The principle of reality, of a word already made flesh and constantly striving to take flesh anew, is essential to evangelization' (*EG*, no. 233).

Made public on 24 November, 2013 at the conclusion to the Year of Faith, but especially on the liturgical Solemnity of Christ the King, this first magisterial document of Francis fully reflects the key point of his spirituality and the direction of his pastoral activity, which is his choice of the mission of Christ, our captain and Lord, who chooses so many individuals and sends them out into the whole world (*EG*, no. 136–148), and his belief that God's Word generate the 'dynamics of "going forth"' in individual believers and in the Church as a whole. The joy of the gospel is in fact a missionary joy which one experiences when one accepts 'this unruly freedom of the word, which accomplishes what it wills in ways that surpass our calculations and ways of thinking' (*EG*, nos 20–24).

2.1 From prophetic hope to the messianic present

The entire Exhortation is punctuated by numerous Scripture references. We will limit ourselves to highlighting the central ones. Francis insists on picking up one of the most authentic traditions in Christian preaching, the one that gives prominence from the beginning until now to its eternal newness: the joyful dimension of the gospel and its proclamation to the world. It is a world which involves not only 'recognizing and discerning spirits but also – and this is decisive – choosing movements of the spirit of good and rejecting those of the spirit of evil' (*EG*, no. 51).[3] Thanks

---

[3] In this regard see the rules for discernment of spirits which Ignatius proposes in the last part of his *SE*, especially nos 313–336.

to the progress achieved in all areas of life, it is a world which can guarantee well-being, but only to some, whereas the majority experience experience precariousness and exclusion. It is a world in which to evangelize also means to acknowledge the challenges coming from consumerism, secularization, the lack of ethics due to the over-emphasis on globalized individualism, the power of seduction of immediate interests which should not rob believers of their missionary vigour (*EG*, no. 109).

The Exhortation takes its lead from some of the many Old Testament texts which express how Israel knew that it must await the joy of messianic salvation even in difficult moments (Is 9:3: 'You have multiplied the nation, you have increased its joy'; cf. also Is 12:6) and how awaiting the coming of the Messiah in hope entails passing on the proclamation to others (Is 40:9: 'Get you up to a high mountain, O herald of good tidings to Zion; lift up your voice with strength, O herald of good tidings to Jerusalem').

For everyone, but especially for the poor, it will be a proclamation of consolation (Is 49:13: 'Sing for joy, O heavens, and exult, O earth! Break forth, O mountains, into singing! For the Lord has comforted his people, and will have compassion on his suffering ones'). The messianic king will proclaim it through his dignity and gentleness (Zech 9:9: 'Rejoice greatly, O daughter of Zion! Shout aloud, O daughter of Jerusalem! Lo, your king comes to you; triumphant and victorious is he, humble and riding on a donkey, on a colt, the foal of a donkey'), and his coming testifies to the fact that God does not give up, even when faced with his people's betrayal (Zeph 3:17: 'The Lord your God is in your midst, a warrior who gives you the victory; he will rejoice over you with gladness, he will renew you in his love; he will exult over you with loud singing, as on a day of festival'). Even on days when things are going badly, the prophet confesses and exhorts: 'the steadfast love of the Lord never ceases … It is good that one should wait quietly for the salvation of the Lord' (Lam 3:22, 26).

The Pope weaves in the wise counsels with the messianic oracles which are aimed at the well-being of people on earth (Sir 14:11, 14: 'My child, treat yourself well, according to your means … Do not deprive yourself of the day's enjoyment'), as well as some incisive notes of his own which echo the voice of the prophets, or wisdom writers: 'I find it thrilling to reread this text' (*EG*, no. 4); 'Why should we not also enter into this great stream of joy?' (*EG*, no. 5); 'What tender, paternal love echoes in these words!' (*EG*, no. 4). There is no claim on Francis' part, then, to make use of Scripture to support his beliefs, as in the era when the Bible was ransacked for *dicta probantia*. Rather is there the exercising of a precise biblical hermeneutics which sees in the joyful expectations of the messianic event, a line of continuation which, as well as uniting Old and New Testaments, supports and illuminates the way for every man and woman on this earth.

As a matter of fact, despite being separated by chronological distance and being connected with very different cultural contexts, the gospel texts are transparent, and without any need to force them, they join prophetic hope with the happy reality of the messianic present. The joy of the gospel, then, is based on the proclamation and fulfilment of the Scriptures realized in Christ, a Messiah who did not come to condemn the world (Jn 3:6), who pardons seventy times seven before asking his disciples to do likewise (Mt 18:21-22, 23-25) and carries the lost sheep on his shoulders (Lk 15:3-7): this is the joy-filled proclamation that musts be communicated to everyone without exception.

2.2 The joy of messianic proclamation

The papal Exhortation strongly emphasizes the fact that the New Testament, at the centre of which shines the glorious cross of Christ, takes up the prophetic tradition and instantly invites us to rejoice for a salvation already present since the beginning of the messianic era. Hence the angel's greeting to Mary: 'Rejoice' (Lk 1:28). Then, following this, it is enough for Mary to greet Elizabeth for her child to leap for joy in Elizabeth's womb (Lk 1:41) and already before being born, the Messiah and the Baptist express the joy of salvation which, like the dawn, bursts into the world through Mary's mouth as she intones her hymn of gratitude to God: 'My spirit rejoices in God my Saviour' (Lk 1:47). Received in faith, then, the divine word is a perennial source of joy for everyone, not just for some, as shown by the proclamation of the birth of the Messiah to the shepherds: 'Do not be afraid: for see – I am bringing you good news of great joy for all the people' (Lk 2:10).

At the beginning of Jesus' ministry, John the Evangelist attributes to the Baptist a reaction filled with exultation for Jesus' messianic ministry (Jn 3:29: 'The friend of the bridegroom, who stands and hears him, rejoices greatly at the bridegroom's voice. For this reason my joy has been fulfilled') while Luke tells us that when Jesus' disciples were sent to proclaim the kingdom of God, they returned full of joy, and 'Jesus rejoiced in the Holy Spirit' because through their mission God has 'hidden these things from the wise and the intelligent and has revealed them to infants' (Lk 10:20-21).

Jesus' message, then, is a source of joy in every situation. As Master and Lord he fully expresses the meaning of his mission by washing his disciples' feet, and after asking them to follow his example, adds: 'If you know these things, you are blessed if you do them' (Jn 13:17). He then insists on the theme of joy even in his final discourse after the Last Supper (Jn 15:11: 'I have said these things to you so that my joy may be in you and that your joy may be complete'), and anticipates the moment of the disciples' distress when he will face death, by confirming them in hope: 'You will have pain but your pain will turn into joy … so you have pain now; but I will see you again and your hearts will rejoice and no one will take your joy from you' (Jn 16:20-22). Finally, just Jesus' resurrection was a reason for profound exultation for the disciples (Jn 20:20: 'Then the disciples rejoiced when they saw the Lord'), so his exultation would be a source of perennial joy for the believers but also an opening to trust in hope for all humankind. According to the Acts of the Apostles, the first community of believers 'ate their food with glad and generous hearts' (Acts 2:42), and when the disciples went around doing good, there was 'great joy in that city' (Acts 8:8) and new converts rejoiced at having believed in God (Acts 8:39; 16:34).

In *EG* no. 10, taking up the Aparecida Document once more, Francis states that 'we discover a profound law of reality,' that is, 'that life is attained and matures in the measure that it is offered up in order to give life to others' and that 'this is certainly what mission means':[4] good tends to communicate, and so also transmitting the *kerygma* is a source of joy given that it involves going to seek what is good for others too. The Apostle Paul, on the other hand, never tires of repeating that acceptance of the *kerygma* is a source of joy: 'Rejoice in the Lord always, again I will say, Rejoice' (Phil 4:4).

In conclusion, in the introductory section of *EG*, Francis lays down the pattern he will then use to weave the plot of his long and well-developed Exhortation. It is a scriptural pattern which highlights the fact that his biblical hermeneutics is based on the texts which transmit in well-defined fashion that from the proclamation of the prophets until the fulfilment of the messianic event in Jesus, only the joyous dimension of the gospel can be the background of the Christian faith and its communication. At the heart of Francis' biblical hermeneutics in *EG* is the belief that only the hope which enlivens and pervades the Judaeo-Christian tradition can make the proclamation of the good news

---

4 5th General Conference of the Latin American and Caribbean Bishops, *Aparecida Document*, (31 May 2007), 360.

efficacious, including in circumstances like today which are especially complex, from both an individual and social point of view, and can meet the many political and religious challenges of our contemporary world.

3. *Laudato Si'*: The world's joyful mystery

Francis himself has given us a glimpse of what might be the biblical filigree of his first Encyclical[5] *Laudato Si': on care for our common home* (*LS*), in his homily for the liturgical Solemnity of Pentecost on the day of its publication: 'Respect for creation is a requirement of our faith: the "garden" in which we live has not been entrusted to us to exploit, but for us to cultivate it and treat it with respect (Gen 2:15). But this is possible only if Adam – the man shaped from the earth – in turn allows himself to be renewed by the Holy Spirit, if he lets himself be refashioned by the Father on the model of Christ the new Adam. Then yes, renewed by the Spirit, we can experience the freedom of children, in harmony with all creation, and in every creature we can recognise a reflection of the Creator's glory as another Psalm says: "O LORD, our Sovereign, how majestic is your name in all the earth!" (Ps 8:1). He guides, renews and gives fruit.'[6]

For the first time, a Bishop of Rome addresses all men and women of the earth with an urgent appeal 'for a new dialogue about how we are shaping the future of our planet'

---

5 Francis also signed the Encyclical *Lumen Fidei* of 29 June 2013, but we know that the text was already largely drawn up by his predecessor, Benedict XVI.

6 Homily at Mass for the Solemnity of Pentecost (24 May, 2015).

(*LS*, no. 14), so that like Francis of Assisi, 'the example par excellence of care for the vulnerable and of an integral ecology lived out joyfully and authentically' (*LS*, no. 10), everyone can 'become painfully aware, to dare to turn what is happening to the world into our own personal suffering, and thus to discover what each of us can do about it' (*LS*, no. 14).

In his *Canticle of the Creatures* the saint from Assisi praised God for the earth: ('Praise be to you, my Lord, through our Sister, Mother Earth, who sustains and governs us, and who produces various fruit with coloured flowers and herbs') thus making evident the paradox that binds living, terrestrial beings to the earth: it is for them at the same time a sister and a mother, a creature like all creatures, which has come from God's hands, but to which God himself has given the task of sustaining and feeding all other creatures. Now, eight centuries later, a pope who has come from one of the places in this world from which the cry arises strongly for this sister who 'cries out to us because of the harm we have inflicted on her by our irresponsible use and abuse of the goods with which God has endowed her' (*LS*, no. 2), asks the world, as John Paul II once did, for a 'complete ecological conversion'[7] to protect our common home which, for believers, reveals something of God himself.[8]

In the introduction (*LS*, nos 15–16), Francis lays down the key elements of his argument, which he then develops

---

7 FRANCIS, Catechesis (17 January, 2001), 4; *Insegnamenti* 24/1 (2001), 179.

8 Cf. Wisdom 13:5: 'When we realize how vast and beautiful the creation is, we are learning about the Creator at the same time'; Rom 1:20: 'Ever since God created the world, his invisible

by following the 'see-judge-act' method practised by the General Conferences of the Latin American and Caribbean Bishops at Medellín, Puebla and Aparecida. We already see this from the titles of the different chapters which deal with 'seeing' that is not neutral because the reality itself is never neutral (*LS*, nos 20-61), of a 'judging' in the light of faith, thus the results of discernment, and of an 'acting' which implies responsibility and dedication.

Aside from some biblical references which punctuate the text, it is in the second chapter (*LS*, nos 62–100) that Francis presents a kind of brief essay on biblical theology. His biblical perspective is clear: reference to Scripture is essential for crossing the middle ground between 'seeing' and 'acting'. Middle ground, but not *terra nullius* because, for the believer, the Bible dominates this ground. 'Judging' in fact means looking at the reality in the light of God's Word, because 'faith convictions can offer Christian, and some other believers as well, ample motivation to care for nature and for the most vulnerable of their brothers and sisters' (*LS*, no. 64), but it also means looking at it in the light of causes for which the earth is like it is today (*LS*, nos 101–136) and, finally, in the perspective of a new eco-anthropological understanding which pursues the common good, in justice (*LS*, nos 137–162).

Much has been said and written on *LS* as the first ecological encyclical in the Church's history, and this is undeniably the case. But this does not mean that it is not

qualities, both his eternal power and his divine nature, have been clearly seen; they are perceived in the things that God has made.'

a strongly theological text, because as Francis said in his homily at Pentecost, 'respect for creation is a requirement of our faith.' In this case too, as with *EG*, he draws from scriptural hermenuetics the theological principle which in fact guides all he has written. From its title until the last chapter, dedicated to education to ecological spirituality (*LS*, nos 202–246), and the two prayers with which the Encyclical concludes, the entire Encyclical is shot through with the belief that for the 'Judeo-Christian tradition the word "creation" has a broader meaning than "nature", for it has to do with God's loving plan in which every creature has its own value and significance' (*LS*, no. 76).

Francis then goes back over the biblical theology of creation, ranging from the original myths of Genesis to the prophetic vision of the Apocalypse, and gives his attention to the earthly Jesus 'in daily contact with the matter created by God,' far removed from the unhealthy dualisms which have 'left a mark on certain Christian thinkers in the course of history and disfigured the Gospel' (*LS*, nos 96–98), as well as to Christ 'risen and glorious, present throughout creation by his universal Lordship' (*LS*, no. 100).

Well aware that the men and women of biblical history had no idea about the ecological question, the Pope insists on the fact that they knew very well that the earth, even with all its hidden dangers, is the garden in which God had placed the human species 'to till it and keep it' (Gen 2:15): the earth is *of* God (Ps 24:1) but *for* mankind (*LS*, no. 67). Instead, for the original accounts, the critical question is the anthropological one of Cain's jealousy (Gen 4:3-8) and the 'wickedness of humankind' which 'was great in the earth' (Gen 6:5). It is also true, however, that the creation accounts 'full of symbolism, bear witness to a conviction which we share today that everything is interconnected, and that genuine care for our own lives and our relationship with nature is inseparable from fraternity, justice and faithfulness to others' *(LS,* no. 70). We cannot deny that the integral ecology which Pope Francis aspires to, an environmental, economic, social and cultural ecology of daily life driven by the principle of the common good and justice between generations (*LS*, nos 137–162) is profoundly inspired by the biblical view of life.

Pope Francis does not use the Bible as if it were a treatise on theodicy, and is not concerned with asking himself how come, if God exists, there is evil in the world. We see evil and it is a manifestation of original sin. His interpretation of the sin-creation relationship, it is true, remains tied to a dated exegesis of the original stories, which deprives them of their outstanding sapiential character. But it is true that for him the main thread of the biblical revelation is not found in sin, which is a kind of introduction to it, but runs rather along a continuum of positive testimonies which testify to the fact that for the Bible, human beings endowed with intelligence can never claim to dominate the earth or any other living being[9] (*LS*, nos 67–69). As for God, 'all it takes is one good person to restore hope' (*LS*, no. 71).

From the way in which Francis links biblical faith and ecological duty, it once again seems that his hermeneutical

---

9 Cf. Gen 2:15: Ps 24:1; Dt 10:14; Lev 25:23; Dt 22:4-6; Ex 23:12.

principle lies in identifying the biblical tradition which in a recurring and ongoing way testifies to the positive dimension open to the hope of human life, making it a solid foundation for his argument. It is by no means a secondary tradition and has a great impact, insisting on the predominance of good. It thus implies an appeal to a likewise positive, trusting and responsible reaction. Thus Francis confirms that his hermeneutical principle has a clear pastoral purpose. He draws a supporting line of thought from Scripture and puts it as the foundation for collective awareness, with a view to encouraging believers, but also all men and women living today on our mistreated earth, to commit to looking after our common home. In the light of the biblical revelation, for him the earth is always something more 'than a problem to be solved,' but 'a joyful mystery to be contemplated with gladness and praise' (*LS*, no. 12).

4. *Amoris Laetitia:* why love is a joy

There is no doubt that the post-synodal Apostolic Exhortation *Amoris Laetitia. On love in the family* (*AL*) is the most discussed of this pontificate's magisterial documents, if not the most discussed of all recent pontificates. Yet it may be the least read. Discussion focuses on some of the pastoral perspectives concerning marriage crises, that is, on twenty-six paragraphs (*AL*, nos. 232–258) and it looks like the other three hundred are of little account; without understanding that these twenty-six paragraphs can be understood only from the structure controlling the whole document, and especially from the significant biblical outline with which Francis opens his long and passionate argument.

We know, on the other hand, that when matters are tackled which have to do with morality, especially sexual morality, they lead either to animated discussion or, more often, silence is preferred.[10] Instead, from the outset of the synodal process, Francis expressed his precise intention that no one in the Church be silenced, convinced that 'the complexity of the issues that arose revealed the need for continual open discussion of a number of doctrinal, moral, spiritual and pastoral questions,' distancing himself from both 'an immoderate desire for total change without sufficient reflection or grounding' and an attitude 'that would solve everything by applying general rules or deriving undue conclusions from particular theological considerations' (*AL*, no. 2).

It is interesting to note that immediately after quoting the Synod's *Relatio Finalis*, saying that 'the Christian proclamation on the family is good news indeed' (*AL*, no. 1), Francis dedicates the entire first chapter to the Bible (*AL*, nos 8–30) in order 'to set a proper tone' (*AL*, no. 6) to his Exhortation. *AL* is his document with the most number of Scripture references.[11] This is one confirmation of his desire to locate his reasoning, which goes into the complexity of the marriage situation, within an extensive scenario wherein the tension between calm realism and ideal inspiration already

---

10   Of great interest, on the relationship between *Amoris Laetitia* and moral theology, is the volume by S GOERTZ-C WITTING (eds), Amoris Laetitia. *Un punto di svolta per la teologia morale?*, San Paolo, Cinisello Balsamo, (MI), 2017.

11   94 quotes from the Old Testament; 102 from the four Gospels; 85 from the rest of the New Testament.

reveals that marriage is like any other deeply human reality. The union between a man and a woman never achieves what men and women across the world would like it to be and to which they sincerely aspire.

It is certainly possible to develop formulas, establish norms, dictate principles, but a biblical theology of marriage follows other paths and does not allow us to model facile theories unless at the cost of reducing the biblical aspect to a scheme which lies quite outside it. The Bible can enlighten and sustain those who choose to commit their lives to one of the most serious of life's adventures, that of the incarnation, or in other words, the dailiness of love's demands. This can be done only by respecting the great variety of situations and stances which it presents, without being afraid of its partiality and ambiguity.

The biblical texts, which tell the story of life and reflect on life, speak of marriage as a reality, not just a subject of discussion.

Thus Francis, in this post-synodal Exhortation, carries out the only work it is possible to do if one wishes to speak, albeit in specifically Christian terms, of a reality which, as well as being at the core of the tension between the ideal and the real, has an extremely complex sociological actuality, at times even a dramatic one, because it is affected by enormous cultural differences, and all too often, painful gender differences and financial difficulties which make it hard to even say the word 'love'.

Francis knows that the ideal and the real co-exist in the Bible without the one claiming to exclude the other, and he knows that there cannot be a biblical theology of marriage which does not respect this ever unresolved tension, because otherwise the ideal becomes overloaded with violence and any prospect of realism is lost.

We cannot take up the entire mosaic of biblical quotations here, which the Pope employs to take account of the biblical view of marriage, bringing together both the 'idyllic picture presented in Psalm 128' and 'a bitter truth found throughout the Sacred scripture' (*AL*, no. 19), concluding by quoting the promise of the Book of Revelation (21:4) that at the end of time, and finally, God 'will wipe away every tear from their eyes' (*AL*, no. 22). We should not miss the fact either, that even the icon of the family at Nazareth, at times presented over-simplistically as the model of inspiration for every Christian family, is described by Francis in terms of 'its daily life [having] its share of burdens and even nightmares' (*AL*, no. 30).

Though in the first chapter the Pope begins with reflection on Psalm 128 and moves within the ambit of Wisdom literature and a handful of New Testament passages, including Matthew's key text on divorce (19:3-9), further on he dedicates a lengthy section of Chapter Four, which deals with 'Love in marriage' (*AL*, no. 89-164), to a meditation on the hymn to charity in St Paul's Letter to the Corinthians, Chapter 13, because 'we cannot encourage a path of fidelity and mutual self-giving without encouraging the growth, strengthening and deepening of conjugal and family love' (*AL*, no. 89). Here, we have a brief essay on biblical exegesis in which Francis enters into the details of the text, examines its terms in the original language and evaluates the author's perspective. He then develops a wise reflection and exhortation suited to family life in which 'we need to cultivate that strength of love which can help us fight every evil threatening it' (*AL*, no. 119) and which is sustained, at times, also by appeal to biblical texts.

One final consideration is needed. Along the lines of what we have observed thus far, including regarding the crucial and painful question of divorce, Francis shows that he knows very well that the Gospel texts are never monodirectional, In *AL*, then, the reference to Mark 10:2-12, in which Jesus' words put another perspective on the value of the Jewish practice of divorce by seeing marriage as part of the plan of creation, occurs only twice and always in quotations from the *Relatio Synodi* of 2014 (*AL*, no. 61) or the *Relatio Finalis* of 2015 (*AL*, no. 71). Instead, Francis prefers to appeal to Matthew's version in the context of the argument with the Pharisees over the Mosaic law in favour of divorce (Mt 19:39). In this, after referring to the initial ideal ('from the beginning it was not so'), the evangelist includes a version of Jesus' saying with an important parenthesis: 'And I say to you, whoever divorces his wife, except for unchastity, and marries another commits adultery.' Francis' comment on this confirms, on the one hand, his deep respect for the biblical text; on the other, his willingness to remain anchored in real life: 'For good reason Christ's teaching on marriage (cf. Mt 19:3-9) is inserted within a dispute about divorce. The Word of God constantly testifies to that sombre dimension already present at the beginning when, through sin, the relationship of love and purity, between man and woman, turns into domination: "Your desire shall be for your husband, and he shall rule over you" (Gen 3:16)' (*AL*, no. 19). No one can deny that Matthew's Gospel effectively demonstrates, including in the question of divorce, that even the first Christian community was able to understand that fidelity to Jesus' Gospel asks us not to renounce the principles but also to also know how to accept that there are exceptions.

As it is with *LS*, the world is 'more than a problem to be solved, it is a joyful mystery to be contemplated with gladness and praise' (*LS*, no. 12), so in *AL*, for Francis, families 'are not a problem; they are first and foremost an opportunity'[12] (*AL*, no. 7). Only a Church which itself, first of all can discern between crises which are 'a new "yes", enabling love to be renewed, deepened and inwardly strengthened' (*AL*, no 235), and some cases in which 'respect for one's own dignity and the good of the children requires not giving in to excessive demands or preventing a grave injustice, violence or chronic ill-treatment' (*AL*, no. 241) can be a Church which knows how to rejoice at the joy of love experienced by families.[13]

5. *Misericordia et Misera:* This is the time for mercy

Wherever or in whatever way people celebrated the Jubilee Year which Francis wanted dedicated to mercy, every believer knows all too well that the word 'mercy' was spoken

---

12 Quoted from *Address at meeting with families in Santiago de Cuba* (22 September 2015), in *L'Osservatore Romano* (in Italian, 24 September 2015, 7).

13 Cf. *AL*, no. 1: 'The joy of love experienced by families is also the joy of the Church'.

often. It challenged, scandalized, encouraged, upset, consoled and irritated people. Of necessity, the question arises: why does mercy create so much fear, and why are we disposed to thinking we don't need it, and even to not showing it?

In reality, 'mercy' is a strong word in the evangelical lexicon, and Pope Francis' Apostolic Letter *Misericordia et Misera* (*MeM*) published at the end of the Holy Year shows this. We need only hope it is not dismissed too quickly, but receives the attention it deserves, also because it brings us to the heart of Francis' magisterium and contributes solidly to highlighting its biblical foundation.

As a key word in the biblical lexicon, 'mercy' runs through all of the experience of the relationship between God and his people, a relationship in which God is viscerally involved, in other words, with the very generative power of a mother (Is 49:15) and the protective instinct of a father (Ps 103:13). Above all, God's visceral love is found in its fullest expression in the person of Jesus: Augustine sums up Jesus' encounter with the woman caught in adultery in just two terms which gave the Pope his title for his Apostolic Letter *MeM*.[14] 'Mercy' points to Jesus himself, his person: he is the embodiment of God's merciful love which goes out to meet the sinner.

Furthermore, as already indicated, Francis wanted to confirm his choice of motto for his episcopate as the choice for his pontificate also – the words with which Bede the Venerable comments on the call of Levi (Matthew) the tax collector: 'Vidit ergo Iesus publicanum et quia miserando

14   In Job 33:5

atque eligendo vidit, ait illi Sequere me.'[15] Tied strongly to his personal experience and Jesuit spirituality, the paired words, *Miserando atque eligendo* refer to the Matthean version of the Gospel episode (Mt 9:9-13) in which, by contrast with the other two Synoptics, the evangelist quotes the prophetic tradition, especially Hosea's words: 'Go and learn what this means, "I desire mercy not sacrifice"' (Mt 9:13). As it was for Matthew, then, 'mercy' is a prophetic word for Francis, questioning a religious system where the privileges of some bring about the forced exclusion of others.

Certainly for Francis, 'mercy' is also a spiritual word, but it takes root in a strong individual interiority which is at the same time self-possessed and outwardly focused, sealed by the prayer *Sume et suscipe* (Take, Lord and receive) which brings the journey of the *SE* to its completion: 'this is sufficient for me' (*SE* 234, 4). Whoever does not understand this switches the evangelical meaning of the term 'mercy' to a dead-end track of sentimental devotion, or it gets lost in useless, senseless discussions on the possibility of keeping mercy and justice together. Instead, for Francis, 'mercy' entails self-awareness and taking on responsibility for others, implies the decision to put freedom, memory, intelligence and will at the disposal of the gospel of mercy.

---

15 In 1953, at the liturgy for the Feast of St Matthew, the eighteen year-old Bergoglio had a profound conversion experience for the first time. His decision to enter the society of Jesus is connected with this. Starting from this, in his first interview given to the editor of *La Civiltà Cattolica*, Antonio Spadaro, Pope Francis claims that the right way of describing who Jorge Mario Bergoglio is, is 'I am a sinner' (cf. interview as recorded on the Holy See website http://w2.vatican.va).

It is a dynamic word, not a prepackaged one, but one which reveals its meanings and possibilities in practice and through discernment.

Francis stakes his entire pontificate on mercy, and wants to give history a Church which feels called to live at a time of mercy and which makes itself a bearer of the culture of mercy. From the outset, the Apostolic Letter which concludes the Jubilee Year, reveals the depth of ecclesiological meaning he attributes to the dimension of mercy, which 'cannot become a mere parenthesis in the life of the Church; it constitutes her very existence, through which the profound truths of the Gospel are made manifest and tangible. Everything is revealed in mercy; everything is resolved in the merciful love of the Father' (*MeM*, no. 1).

'Mercy' is a 'theo'-logical word, that is, it 'speaks of God' and says who God is, beginning with what God does. It is a word of biblical theology, then, before being one of dogmatic theology. It is a christological word, the Christology of the Gospels, before being a Nicene or Chalcedonian word. It is a word which configures the Church and commits it to the world, because it always goes beyond not just a 'worldly' way of thinking, but 'the world's' way of thinking.

MeM is an exhortative and prescriptive Letter. It is aimed at faith practice, the life of the community. With it, Francis sought to spell out the new agenda for the life of all local Churches for which, before God, he also bears responsibility. It is an agenda which gives attention to liturgy and sacramental life, to hearing the Word, to the Sacrament of Reconciliation, the ministry of consolation which is to be prophetically proclaimed in life and at the death of each and every person. It gives attention especially to families, to the 'creativity of mercy' in the public space, the capacity, in other words, to invent ever new testimonies of mercy like, for example, the World Day of the Poor which Francis insisted be celebrated throughout the Church. It is an agenda with roots in a 'pastoral conversion' shaped daily by the renewing strength of mercy. In fact for Francis, mercy is not a topic or subject like any other, adapted to a Holy Year, but the theological foundation of the life of faith. Perhaps it is really because of this that the message of mercy is such a serious and demanding one. However, it is the unique, true, good news, the unique gospel of Jesus of Nazareth.

One last observation. We said earlier that Francis has understood that in the life of the Church, the service of the Word and the service of charity can never be separated. He has understood it and puts it into practice in such a way that life and Scripture establish the hermeneutical criteria for each other. It is no coincidence, then, that in his Apostolic Letter *MeM*, he asks the Church to dedicate two separate Sundays of the Liturgical Year to the Word and to charity respectively.

On the one hand, each community is invited, on one Sunday in the Liturgical Year, 'to renew its efforts to make the Sacred scriptures better known and more widely diffused' (*MeM*, no. 7). On the other, as a further concrete sign that mercy is something which goes beyond a Holy Year, the whole Church is asked to celebrate the World Day of the Poor on the 33rd Sunday in Ordinary Time. The reasons Francis offers as the basis for this celebration once again requires that the Church convert, and also convert the significance it has given to the liturgical celebration of Christ the King, and to the letter of the gospel, for which 'Our Lord Jesus Christ, King of the Universe ... identified with the little ones and the poor, and who will judge us on our works of mercy (cf. Mt 25:31-46)' (*MeM*, no. 21).

IN CONCLUSION

Perhaps there is no need to add further words to the many already said. Pope Francis' biblical hermeneutics presumes an understanding of Scripture which starts out from life, and an understanding of life which starts out from Scripture. This allows him to grasp hold of a proclamation within the biblical text which opens life up to hope.

Sustained by a strong Ignatian spirituality, Francis' biblical interpretation has a prophetic vigour which enables it to challenge and judge, but also console and support. This is how it translates into proclamation. He knows all too well that *thinking with the Church* means being obedient to what that Spirit is telling the Church, and so he takes the legacy of Vatican Council II seriously, putting service of the Word at the centre, and drawing from it the gospel to be announced to the poor.

On the other hand, Francis knows his Church and knows that like all other religious institutions, there are those in it 'who ultimately trust only in their own powers and feel superior to others because they observe certain rules or remain intransigently faithful to a particular Catholic style from the past. A supposed soundness of doctrine or discipline leads instead to a narcissistic and authoritarian elitism, whereby, instead of evangelizing, one analyzes and classifies others, and instead of opening the door to grace, one exhausts his or her energies in inspecting and verifying' (*EG*, no. 94).

Despite this, he pushes on, convinced that the strong words around which God's dialogue with human beings is woven throughout history are *gaudium, laus, laetitia, misericordia*. This is a biblical lexicon that only one with ears to hear can understand. It is a lexicon which from the beginning, as well as winning over many to the following of the Prophet of Nazareth, irritated and scandalized many others who ended up lifting him up on a cross. This is because it is a lexicon which goes to the heart of faith wherein lies the crucial question: 'Where is your God?' (Ps 42:4).

It is a question which each individual is called to provide an answer to, yet Francis' invitation is clear: 'If you want to see God's face, look in the Bible.' His magisterium is testimony that for him 'the Bible is the great story of the marvels of God's mercy. Every one of its pages is steeped in the love of the Father who from the moment of creation wished to impress the signs of his love on the universe. Through the words of the prophets and the wisdom writings, the Holy Spirit shaped the history of Israel as a recognition of God's tenderness and closeness, despite the people's infidelity. Jesus' life and preaching decisively marked the history of the Christian community, which has viewed its mission in terms of Christ's command to be a permanent instrument of his mercy and forgiveness (cf. Jn 20:23). Through Sacred Scripture, kept alive by the faith of the Church, the Lord continues to speak to his Bride, showing her the path she must take to enable the Gospel of salvation to reach everyone. I greatly desire that God's word be increasingly celebrated, known and disseminated, so that the mystery of love streaming from the font of mercy may be ever better understood. As the Apostle tells us clearly, "All Scripture is inspired by God and profitable for teaching, for reproof, for correction, and for training in righteousness' (2 Tim 3:16)"' (*MeM*, no. 7).

www.ingramcontent.com/pod-product-compliance
Lightning Source LLC
Chambersburg PA
CBHW052028290426
44112CB00014B/2421